TWENTY-ONE TALES OF HARBLEDOWN

Ron Pepper was born in Canterbury and now lives in Harbledown. He attended the Simon Langton Boys School and went on to Exeter College, Oxford to read for a degree in Geography. In 1964 he was awarded an M.A. degree by London University for a thesis in urban historical geography. A retired senior Schools Inspector, Ron spent much of his working life as a geography teacher and then a headteacher in south London comprehensive schools.

On returning to the Canterbury area he used his early retirement to follow up, among other things, a long-standing interest in local history and archaeology. He studied for a Diploma in Archaeology at the University of Kent, doing extensive research into the environmental location of East Kent's Iron Age settlements, as well as taking part in various archaeological "digs" in Canterbury.

Drawing together these threads of local historical knowledge and experience, Ron has turned to fiction-based-on-fact as a way of sharing his enthusiasm with a wider audience.

When not reading, writing, organising Adult Education classes for the W.E.A. or taking part in local political or voluntary organisation activity, Ron enjoys the company of his wife Jane and family, including five grand-daughters.

Twenty-one Tales
of
Harbledown

by

Ron Pepper

Best wishes

Ron Pepper

Buckland Publications Ltd.
125 High Holborn, London WC1V 6QA

First Published 1995

ISBN 0 7212 0884 3

Printed and bound in Great Britain by
Buckland Press Ltd., Dover, Kent.

CONTENTS

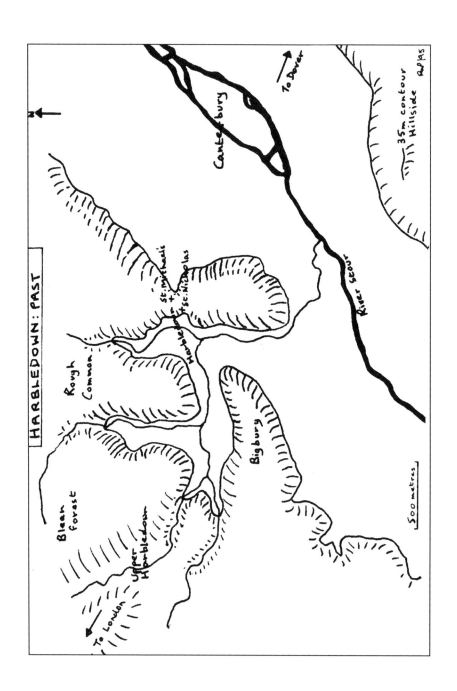

HARBLEDOWN: PAST

To London
Blean Forest
Upper Harbledown
Rough Common
St. Michael
St. Nicholas
Harbledown
Bigbury
Canterbury
To Dover
River Stour
35m contour Hillside
500 metres

N

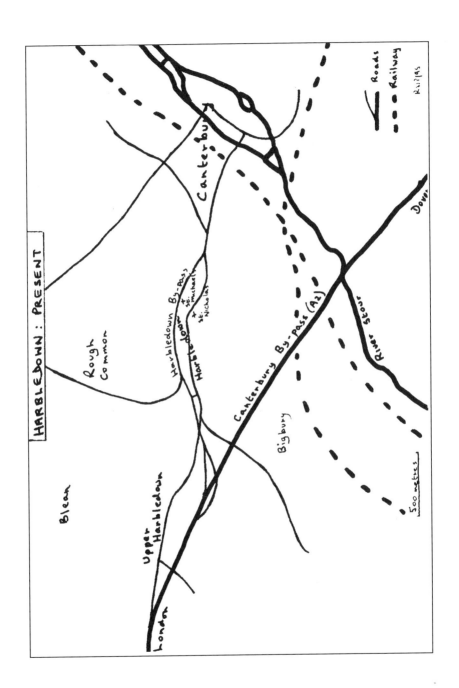

HARBLEDOWN : PRESENT

Blean

Upper Harbledown

London

Rough Common

Harbledown By-Pass

St. Michael's
St. Nicholas

Harbledown

Canterbury

Canterbury By-Pass (A2)

Bigbury

River Stour

Dover

Roads
Railway
Bypass

500 metres

INTRODUCTION

The histories of Harbledown and Canterbury are inevitably intertwined. Less than a mile apart, Harbledown sits high on the valley side, overlooking the city. Today Harbledown comprises three distinctive localities: the original Lower Harbledown; Upper Harbledown half a mile away, now beyond the village by-pass; and the newer, much expanded Rough Common, up against the edge of the ancient Blean forest. The sparsely settled Bigbury hilltop makes up the fourth part, located the other side of the thundering A2 by-pass which sweeps past Canterbury.

These four components have a total population of just over two thousand, more than double that of sixty years ago and increasingly incomers, people who have chosen to live in a place redolent with history, near enough to Canterbury to use its many facilities, far enough away to have a local sense of identity if not community. The essential quality of Harbledown is its variety, small, steep hills, winding roads and lanes, houses of different ages and styles, two ancient churches, orchards and fields, streams and undulating vales, high, windy meadows with vast panoramic views and, above all, trees.

Trees cover the distant hump of the Bigbury hill-fort, trees dominate the skyline to the north, the ancient Blean forest, trees edge the orchards and hop-gardens and streams, trees in gardens, in the churchyards, along the roadsides. The ancient power of the forest, the wild-wood, which once covered all of the land, is ever present. Humankind has lived on and farmed this land for at least five thousand years and was here before that, but perhaps just passers-by. Bigbury pre-dates Canterbury as a major settlement but is now, for the city-dwellers, much out of sight and out of mind.

There is no definitive history of Harbledown separate from that of Canterbury, nor is there likely to be. There are random, tantalising snippets of information, passing references, scattered archaeological finds, reminiscences which in themselves provide not much more than hints for speculation. Put these in the context of Canterbury's history, even national history, and a greater coherence begins to emerge. To try to give flesh to history's dry bones by inventing characters and stories, weaving fact with fiction, is a risk, but if it helps make some sense of the continuity of a place and its people, then it's worthwhile.

Each of the following tales attempts to set Harbledown in the framework of what was happening in Canterbury and the wider national scene. Inevitably, with a place that has two ancient churches less than four minutes' walk apart, there is a strong under-current of religious influences on events, reflected in the stories. Most of the main characters are imagined, but not all, and they are intended to suggest how the comings and goings of the great, the good (and the bad) impinged upon the local people and their environment. After centuries of slow change the pace and pressure for new developments is accelerating. For Harbledown the next few years will be critical if it is to retain its unique character, hence the 'cautionary tale' set in A.D. 2020, less than a generation away.

Only by knowing the past can we understand the present and only by understanding the present can we influence the future. Not an original thought, but one I would commend to you.

Ron Pepper,
September, 1994.

TALE ONE

Cold Comfort

Some nine thousand years ago the place we call Harbledown was part of mainland Europe for the English Channel had not yet appeared. It was soon after the last major Ice Age, and to the north, the glaciers were in retreat, with the climate gradually warming and the forests slowly marching in to cover the land. By now our local area was thickly forested with pine and birch trees, with oak, ash and alder on the increase. In this unbroken carpet of wild-wood lived wild ox, red deer, roe deer and wild pig as well as bears and wolves. The local hills stood higher than today with fast-flowing streams cutting into their flanks, thickly covered by wind-deposited soils. These small watercourses headed down to a wide river, our Stour, itself busy swinging back and forth, carving out a broad, swampy valley. Humans were few and lived by hunting and gathering, sometimes travelling far into the great green wilderness, following the seasonal migrating herds . . .

Mageven shivered and crouched closer to the spluttering fire. He pulled the pelt tighter round his shoulders, hunkering down with his back to the cold, dusty wind keening up over the hill. He was waiting for the rest of the hunting party of six men and their dogs to return. They had chosen this high spot to camp on as it gave a good view out over the wide valley where the swampy marshland promised a fine catch of water-birds.

Already the season was late-on. The forest leaves were yellowing to brown, the great flocks of birds swiftly moving south. Even now the sun was sinking fast behind the wooded ridge to the west, a great red disc casting long, deep shadows across the land. Mageven poked restlessly at the fire with a stick, urging it to flame higher, wishing the others would hurry back soon. He had been left behind to keep watch over the temporary camp, alone with not even one of the dogs to keep him

11

company. Two days before he had twisted his ankle whilst chasing a deer, driving it towards the hunters crouched in the undergrowth, their flint-tipped spears at the ready. He felt foolish because he prided himself on being swift and surefooted. Still, his crash and cry had startled the deer on to his waiting kin and another fine skin was stretched out to dry. They had eaten well that night.

So far this had been a good hunting trip. They had moved north to this place, walking for two full hands of days, crossing the vast valley lowland, with its rivers and marshes, one day to be covered by the sea – or so the old wise-one had foretold.

As they worked their way through the open forest lands, skirting the edge of the high hills, they had followed ancient trackways, marked out by significant features in the landscape – a round-topped hill, a sharp river bend – and memorised by chanting every night round the camp-fire. It was not enough to be a skilled hunter and tracker, much more knowledge was needed to survive. What plants, berries and nuts were edible, what were for curing ailments and wounds; how to shape the flint-stone for blades, hand axes and tools; how to skin and smoke the carcasses; how to make fire; and how to live with the land and to revere it.

Along the way they had camped and left caches of skins and pelts to collect on their way back. But this was their main camp and here they were to stay for one whole moon cycle. It would soon be time to leave.

The hunting around had been good but winter sometimes came early and it would be dangerous to be caught far from the home-camp by early snows. Mageven's father had nearly been trapped two winters before and only he and three others of his party had made it back, leaving behind most of their take to travel more lightly and swiftly. For Mageven this was his first long hunt and for him it marked manhood. This would be his thirteenth winter and to travel so far and return would confirm him as a true hunter. He had learned much, not least how to harbour his strength as the party loped along through the woods, pausing rarely to rest, ever alert, ever ready to freeze still at the raise of an arm. Not that they feared the creatures of the forest, except the great bears, but the hunter's skill required quick reactions like the beasts they tracked.

Now, however, as he fed more kindling on to the fire, he felt alone and afraid. He reached down for the smooth, round pebble that had caught his eye earlier in the day. It was unusually coloured, a shiny reddish-yellow with a small pit in its centre. To while away the waiting he had taken a sharp flint fragment left-over from Galag the tool-maker's knapping and had worked away at the pebble's centre, trying to bore a hole through. It would make a fine charm for his younger brother. But it was slow work and the cold soon began to numb his fingers. His mind began to drift off into the dream-state.

Suddenly Mageven sat upright, his hand reaching for his spear. All his senses were awake. He stayed as still as a rock, his ears straining for that new sound. But all he could hear was the low howl of the wind, the creak of branches, the swish of leaves and the hissing of the fire. Slowly, slowly he eased himself upright, eyes darting around the clearing. Moving silently, he backed up against the broad trunk of the big oak tree. "Always protect your back," he remembered his father saying. His left hand slid forward to grasp a burning brand from the fire.

Now, wait.

There, across to the right, a scuffle of dry leaves, a deep-throated panting sound. And again, silence.

Mageven felt the fear rise in him. Was it a great bear? He tried to breathe slowly and evenly to calm his racing heart. "Where are the others?" he thought desperately, "why don't they come?"

He had known fear before in his young life, when the mighty sky-god roared and thundered above, when the wolves howled around the winter home-camp, when the mid-winter dark pressed in and they waited for the sun to be reborn. But nothing like this. Always, before, there had been the warmth and comfort of his parents and kinfolk, a hand to clasp on to. Now he was a man-hunter and stood alone for the first time.

He bit his lip to stop it trembling – hard until he could taste blood.

The silence went on but he stayed upright, ready. Then, over to the left came another sound, grating, grunting, like teeth grinding together. A tusked boar? Far off, an owl hooted, high and lonely. The dark began to press in on him. Still he held his ground, his spear-hand now sweaty but cold. "Cold fear," he remembered his father telling him. "Turn it into a weapon, use it."

Slowly, slowly he lowered the spear butt into the soft earth at his feet, angling the flint-head chest-high away from him. Even more slowly he began to wave the burning brand, now giving little flame, back and forth, fanning it into brightness. Suddenly he hurled it over to the right, at the same time scooping up another brand and letting out a mighty shout which echoed across the valley.

The second burning branch went out to the left, then another to the right. He felt his heart pound. This was it.

But still, silence.

Then he heard a great bellow of laughter from behind him and suddenly, all around him, were his kinfolk, his father, his older brother, the others, all whooping and hugging in a swirl of affection and joy.

"Welcome to the world of the hunter," his father said, pulling him into a rib-crushing hug. "You have passed the test, you are now a true man, one who can walk alone, stand tall and hold his ground. See what we have for you."

And with that he draped a fresh-hunted bear skin around Mageven's shoulders whilst his brother held out a thong on which were threaded two boar tusks, a powerful charm.

Mageven fought back his tears of joy and, if truth be told, of relief. But he was now a real hunter and hunters only wept for death. This had been his testing time and he had proved himself.

That night he slept well, content and warm beneath his bear skin. The next day they broke camp and began the long trek home. In the excitement Mageven forgot all about the strange stone he had been working on. It remained, awaiting to be found by another.

This is an imagined account of a Mesolithic hunting party camping at Harbledown. Archaeological evidence indicates such hunting groups stayed at temporary camps having likely come across the Channel land bridge, penetrating into southern Britain. No such campsites have yet been found locally but there are skimpy, tantalising hints here and there indicating human presence in the district back in the Mesolithic period.

TALE TWO

The Moon Festival

As the climate became warmer and the seas rose, so new ways of life became possible. The techniques of farming, of planting and tending and reaping, of domesticating sheep, goats and cattle, gradually spread into Europe from the east, eventually crossing the now opened English Channel. With the new way of living came new ideas of ritual and worship, of settling in communities, of collective endeavour based on changed social customs. And likely, an enhanced status for women, the domesticators. Now, some four thousand years ago, our Harbledown area bore the imprint of organised human activity. Patches had been cleared in the still all-embracing oak, ash and beech forest, with small ditch-enclosed fields for grain and paddocks for livestock, for clusters of timber and rush huts. Linking trackways cut down to the streams and the nearby riverside grazing lands. Some of the hilltops had been cleared to become holy places, high and open to the sky. Smoke rose above the clearings, the clunk of flint-head axes chopping into trees echoed around, mixing with the shouts of children and the sounds of cattle and sheep. Humankind was here to stay, rooted in the soil but ever aware of the changing seasons, the sun, the sky and the magical moon . . .

Ayla shifted painfully to ease the ache in her back. Having lived forty summers she was, she reckoned, too old for this knee-cracking, back-ricking corn grinding, rolling the stone back and forth on the grooved quern. It was time she was given more respect by the younger women. After all, once the old wise-woman Uma died, she, Ayla would take her place. Then they would see.

The kin family was small, just four round, wood-post huts with reed and daub walls and thatched roofs, close but not too close to each other, on a good sheltered site. They were well protected from the cold north winds but high enough to overlook the swampy valley below. It was a well-drained and dry place, especially for the sunken corn-store pits. Her folk had lived and farmed here now for many generations, back to the time when this land was thickly forested. They still needed to fight back the woods that pressed in on them but they knew enough to let the soil rest, to gain some new land by clearing whilst letting other patches slip back to the trees for a few seasons.

The ditch-enclosed farmsteads stood close by an ancient trackway which led down to the ford-crossing of the marshy river. They had their own small stream nearby for water. The ford track descended past the midden-heap, and along the edge of the small, rectangular paddocks and fields where they kept their sheep and shaggy cattle and grew their corn and flax. Sometimes the men and boys walked down to the river marshes to fish or hunt for wildfowl, with the women and girls collecting eggs, reeds and rushes and edible roots. The wide woods gave them good hunting for deer and wild boar as well as wolves and bears. It was also a source for kindling and timber for building, and a rich stock of nuts, berries, roots and herbs. These last were for the women to collect for they carried, mother to daughter, the knowledge of remedies for ailments and wounds, what eased aches and pains, what lightened the spirits, what took one into the dream world, and what helped the journey to death.

All this Ayla held in her mind together with how to make fire, how to cook, weave, cure and soften hides, what seeds to plant and when, how to make clay pots, the mysteries of child-birth, the moon rituals. The knowledge needed for tree-clearing, flint-napping, looking after the cattle and sheep, hunting, fishing and, occasionally, fighting, was for the men and boys; and the Sun rites. But Ayla knew, as did the other women, that without their wisdom the men would be nothing but hunters and herders, always on the move, fighting amongst themselves for land and cattle.

To stay in one place, to put down roots, to live in balance and harmony with the Earth Mother meant peace and a good life.

Ayla, like most of her people, was short, slender but well-muscled, with dark brown hair. She wore a simple kirtle, tied in at the waist. Round her neck was a string of black jet beads, a bonding gift of twenty-eight summers ago, given her by her man's mother, now long dead and buried in a circular pit over on the holy hill. She scooped up the last grain heads and put them carefully in the round clay pot. "That's enough for now," she thought. "Time to prepare for tonight's moon festival."

She and the other women of the kin family had already been fasting since the previous day's sun-up, taking only sips of water from time to time. This was to ensure their bodies were purified for the great event, their event, the rising of the harvest moon. Now, as the afternoon sun began its slow descent, the women and girls, nine in all, gathered together in the old wise-woman's small hut. The men folk and boys had, according to the ritual, been driven away until nightfall. This was none of their business.

Chatting quietly amongst themselves they began painting their bodies and faces, using clay pastes, coloured with earths, plant juices and their own blood. They had each brought with them their long, cloak-like gown to wear, plain linen for the women, dyed pale-yellow for the girls. The younger girls had earlier picked bunches of bright late summer flowers which were plaited into hair-garlands. Soon, as the shadows lengthened, Uma, the old wise-woman said it was time to go. They helped her to her feet and together, now chanting a song, they began the slow walk along the hill-crest to the holy place. Here, high up above the valley, they could see out over the land in a great sweep from where the sun rose to where it set, a land of wooded hills and ridges, of gently undulating vales and the wide expanse of the river marshes, with the now-darkening forest cut here and there by farmstead clearings.

Other groups of women from nearby neighbouring homesteads joined them, their voices rising in a powerful flow of sound. They gathered in a wide semi-circle, with the wise-woman from each family group in the centre, all holding hands, looking to the east, out over the shadow-filled valley below. Away, in a sheltered spot, the very young girls looked after the babies, all soundly asleep, well sedated by the special sleep potion.

The men and boys arrived, nervously standing back, away from the semi-circle, the half-moon shape, quiet but restless. The local clan headman, from over on the great ridge hill, stood with the other clan fathers. They wore their showy ceremonial furs, much too hot for this windless evening. They each carried their symbol of power, fine well-polished flint axe-hammers, marvellous to look at but used only for show. Each of these axes carried within it the male spirit, embodying the means of hunting, clearing the trees and defending the clan family. The clan chief's axe was even more special, traded on to him two summers ago, from across the great water it was said. This axe was two-hands long with a thick head-end thinning down to a fine point, highly polished and smooth, made of a hard blue-green stone unknown in these parts.

It was great magic.

The singing stopped for, there, over the far hills, the great yellow-red disc of the harvest moon began to rise. The men and boys fell to their knees, their heads bowed, silent. The women and girls began a slow, weaving circular dance, chanting and smiling with joy. The Moon Goddess had come again in all her glory and was still theirs. The slow, mesmeric rhythm went on and on, feet thudding out a measured beat. Meanwhile the wise-women lit a fire in the centre of the circle and began throwing onto it handfuls of secret herbs, so that sweet smoke filled the air, intoxicating, joy-bringing smoke. Far away, over the valley another hilltop fire sparked into the night sky, then another.

The men and boys began to dance, a log-drum taking up the rhythm, the beat speeding up. Soon the hilltop was alive with dancers, twisting, turning, leaping and weaving in and out, but still holding the moon-circle shape.

Suddenly a cloud blacked out the moon, now riding high. The dancing ceased abruptly and a great moan of anguish went up, echoing across the valley. All was totally dark, except for the fire at the heart of the circle. This was a bad omen. But the wise-women knew what to do. From them arose a new chant, a wailing cry which rose and fell in the darkness. All the other folk fell to their knees, waiting, silent, recognising the song for what it was, the song of sacrifice. The fire flared up and a loud voice called, "Ayla, come forth."

Ayla stood and walked slowly to the fire. There, on the ground lay Uma, stretched out straight, her face relaxed and smiling for she was the one who had gone to meet the Moon Goddess, helped on her way by a sharp, thin-bladed flint knife to the heart. This year it was her turn, the oldest and most precious gift they could offer. Other years it might be a wrong-doer, or a young crippled child, or another, like Uma, whose time had come to make the journey.

"Ayla, join us. You are now the wise-woman for your kin family. Take Uma's place, for she has gone to join our big sister in the sky."

Ayla raised her arm to the heavens and then, as was right, the great black cloud slid away, revealing the Moon Goddess in her shining glory. All was well, the future was assured, the celebrations could continue. And Ayla was well pleased.

"Now those younger women will see who really knows what's best, for I am now wise-woman. No more corn-grinding for me, that's for sure."

The celebrations began again, now with feasting and drinking the intoxicating brew, prepared earlier by the women. Whole sheep and pigs roasted in the crackling fire-pits, laid the previous day. The men were allowed that particular chore.

There was one final ritual for that night. As the moon began her slow slide down behind the hill it was time for Ayla to meet the clan chief Gurum and pledge herself and her wisdom to all. As the darkness began to fade so the feasting, dancing and chanting ceased, family groups, men and women, boys and girls coming together. The fire was built up high, crackling and flaming into the sky. Soon the first rays of dawn would show eastwards –the sun would return.

After a certain amount of feet shuffling and huffing and puffing, the family headmen arranged themselves around Gurum. The chief wizard, the clan's priest-magician, a scrawny old man dressed in assorted pelts and feathers, stepped forward into the circle of firelight. He called for silence.

Gurum joined him, holding the shiny, blue-green axe-hammer in both hands, stretched out before him at arm's length. Ayla knelt at his feet and reached forward, placing both palms of her hands on the cold stone, pledging herself to the clan. She felt the power of the axe tingle through her palm, up her arms, to and through her whole body. This was indeed a magic axe but deep in the core of her mind she remembered the words of her own mother, Uma. "These men think they hold the power of life and death, but without us and our wisdom they would be lost and useless. Never forget."

And she didn't.

Evidence for Neolithic settled farming has been found across the Harbledown district, not least near the top of Summer Hill, the home of the imagined Ayla. The jadeite axe, a prestige symbol, thought to have come originally from Brittany, was "found in the Canterbury area". The suggested ceremonial hilltop holy site is now on the upper edge of the London Road estate, just along from Summer Hill. The harvest moon ritual is rooted deep in the past of many cultures; there is archaeological evidence from this period which suggests ritual human sacrifice was practiced.

TALE THREE

Bigbury Beginnings

The way of life of the Neolithic farmers seems to have changed little over nearly two thousand years. New religious customs emerged as did a different social organisation; providing the massive communal efforts needed to build the linear long barrows and ritual ways and the circular henges and barrows, turning whole areas into huge ritual landscapes. With the gradual and increasing use of metals, copper, then bronze, then iron, came perhaps a shift to a more male-dominated, violent society. In the Iron Age, down to around 600 B.C. the climate deteriorated, becoming wetter and colder, with shorter growing-seasons, and cattle became increasingly a measure of wealth. The Iron Age, the time of the Celtic warrior-chieftain had arrived. Forests still dominated our local landscape. The rivers and streams flowed on; the seas slowly rose; humans came and went but the hills remained unchanged except where defensive hill-forts had emerged to impress the clanfolk and deter the foe. The Harbledown area stayed largely unaltered but where, for whatever reasons, the humans left, the wild-wood quickly reclaimed the land . . .

Calyad trudged on through the whispering, deepening snow, his head bowed against the biting north wind and stinging ice-flakes. He and his three companions were following the old trackway, running high along the river valley side, heading north-eastwards. It was early in the winter for such a storm and he knew they soon needed to find shelter before nightfall. As it was, the light was fading fast, lost in a whirling white mist of snowflakes. They stayed close, single-file, each keeping the man in front in sight. Except for the lead man.

The track, much overgrown, led through thick woods which gave some, but little, shelter, for the wind howled and keened through the bare

21

branches. Calyad's feet and hands, although well swathed, were numb with cold, icicles fringed his beard, eyebrows and nostrils. "This is not good," he thought. "Bad enough to have to travel so far this late in the season, but in such cold . . ." He found his thoughts drifting away, another sign the cold was seeping into him.

Suddenly the lead man held up an arm, halting the party. Through the swirling snow they could just make out they had reached a rough, open patch and there, over to the right, was a low hump, overgrown with bushes.

"This will do," said Calyad. "We'll shelter here."

The weary travellers shuffled over to the mound, pushing their way into the dense bushes, stamping out a small, sheltered circle. The first need was a fire but even with Calyad's skill with the fire-stones this took some time to get going, the dry moss and twigs they brought with them continually spluttering and dying out before, at last, a flame caught. Soon a warming fire flickered and flared and the men were able to squat round it, huddled together for warmth. They managed to heat up some of the deer meat they carried though it became charred in the process.

The group had travelled far, walking now for ten days, searching, seeking for a new home. They came from the west, dispossessed of their lands by a raiding clan who had stormed their chief's hilltop enclosure, taking many warrior heads, making slaves of the women and children and stealing the clan's wealth, their cattle. Calyad and his kinsfolk of four families had, fortunately for them, not been able to reach the chief's enclosure before the attack. They lived at the furthest edge of the clan territory and by the time the summoning had reached them it was all over. They had seen the glow in the sky as the chief's family huts burnt, so withdrew to the shelter of the thick woods, unsure what to do. If they remained for too long in hiding their food would likely run out and they would then have to throw themselves on the mercy of the raiders from the north – slavery or starvation, not much of a choice they decided. These were indeed difficult times, with tribes on the move, pushed by hunger as a series of harvests failed due to wet springs and cloudy summers. At such times the strong man, the warrior leader, came into his own, taking his young fighters on raids, ever further distant, seeking cattle, corn and slaves – and places where the living was easier. For the warriors the chance to take the head of a foe as a trophy was an added incentive.

So it came about that Calyad and the four others made their journey, travelling into the empty eastlands, to find a new home. They had heard few people lived in these parts for it had long been cursed with a sickness which killed without mercy. For generations now travellers from the east had been given a wide berth, but Calyad had noticed the ones he saw looked healthy enough. He persuaded the others, after a full debate amongst the families with much arguing back and forth, that there was no other way but to send a small scouting party to find out what lay in the lands where the sun rose. If all was well, two would stay, the others return and lead the families to a new life. On the journey they had already lost one of their number, a young man who had missed his footing crossing a swift-running river and been swept away. And then the snowstorm had struck. These were bad signs.

The night passed, long, uncomfortable and cold. They took it in turns to sleep, one always awake to keep the fire going and guard against danger. Once, in the far distance, they heard wolves howling. By dawn the storm had abated, the snow had stopped and the skies began clearing. It was time to decide what to do. In a way, the decision was made for them because they quickly noticed, now it was light, that the low bushy mound they had camped on was an old homestead hut site and that the glade in which it stood had once been a small, ditch-bounded field, kept clear of tree-growth probably by grazing deer. People had lived here before, and if then, why not again?

They agreed to split up in pairs and explore around and about, meeting back at midday. Calyad set off with Maroc, his sister's husband, a wiry man with sharp senses. They headed off to the left-hand of the glade, the other two to the right. The soft snow creaked underfoot as they forced their way through the trees and bushes. Maroc noticed that many of the trees here were mature but not really ancient, suggesting the land had once been cleared and then abandoned, the forest gradually reclaiming its own.

Suddenly they broke through the trees and found themselves standing on the edge of a deep drop, the land falling away, giving them a wide view out across a snow-covered countryside of small wooded hills and vales, backed in the near-distance by a high, flat hill-line which ran from east to west. They could easily pick out the courses of several streams as the sun glinted back from the water. "An easy place to defend," Maroc ventured. "And water close to hand as well. I wonder what the soil's like?"

Calyad gestured to the right. "Look, this hilltop bears round. Let's follow the edge."

Picking their way carefully along the hill-crest they found they were heading first eastwards but gradually bearing round. Below them the slope continued to fall away to gently undulating land. Suddenly Maroc pointed. "Look, there, to the right of that high hill. A wide river valley. That's the one we've been skirting for the past two days. I reckon we're on a ridge end, with steep sides all round except where the trackway comes from. And look, there, below, you can just make out the track heading for that hill. Likely an old holy place up top."

Just then they heard and recognised a loud curse and a bellow of laughter. It was their companions, one of whom had slipped and sat himself down in a patch of wet slush. By now the snow was melting fast, with soft, wet lumps plopping down from the tree branches above. Lyef and Agar reported what they had seen. On their side of the ridge the land dropped away, more gently it seemed, down to the river valley bottom. From what they could make out along the river were flood plain marshes and meadows suggesting good summer grazing for cattle. And there was another trackway leading down towards the river. "Must be a ford," said Maroc thoughtfully. "And if that track heads on east it must come to the great wide water we've been told about. Where the traders come from. If the soil's good, then this might be the place. There's no sign of anyone else living hereabouts, no smoke in the sky."

They went back to the old clearing and made up the fire again. It gave them a focus around which to sit and talk, and was a tradition they carried on almost without thinking. It was what you did when important matters needed discussing. They went through the advantages and disadvantages of this place: it was very easy to defend and keep watch over the surrounding countryside; the trees gave good shelter and would provide timber for building, for fire-making and for tools; there was water, close by, downslope. The thick forests away to the north promised good hunting but also a hiding place for intruders. The river offered fishing, wildfowl, reeds and rushes and perhaps easy access to the sea. By the look of the flatness on either bank there would be good summer grazing. Downhill the land looked easy to clear and plough and if the soils were good, as Maroc again reminded them, they could expect . harvests of corn. Then there were the trackways; they could be both a blessing and a danger. "Any traders passing through will have to come this way. But then any raiders from the west would come straight on top of us," said Calyad. "There is a way though. If we dig a dyke, a ditch across the neck of this ridge, from steep side to steep side, then, with enough of us, we could block out any intruders." The others nodded their agreement.

"Let's go look at the soil down below," insisted Maroc. They walked

24

down the steep, slippery hillside to the gently undulating lands at the ridge foot. Maroc bent, brushed the snow aside and scratched out a handful of frozen earth. Warming it in his hands, he then rubbed it between his fingers, smelled it, tasted it. "This is good," he said – and from him that was enough.

The only other concern which nibbled at their minds was about the spirits of those who had lived here before. Was this a wholesome place, was there any evil lurking about? Would they be welcomed here by the local god-beings? They talked this one through, concluding they had been guided to this spot, that it felt right and had been waiting for them.

So they decided. Here would be the new home place.

The next day Lyef and Agar began the long trek back to bring the families. Travelling light and fast they could make it in five or six days; the return, with the old and young and the livestock would take much longer. Meanwhile, Calyad and Maroc set to work, first to build shelter against the coming winter, then digging out a pond they lined with clay in which to store water. They hacked back the undergrowth and enlarged the clearing, creating a paddock for the livestock. A great pile of branches was stacked, fuel for the fires. Then, when the basic work had been done, they started in to cut the dyke, a slow, hard labour for just the two, but a beginning. It took until the next midsummer, when everyone from the families had helped, to finish, but finished it was. Bigbury had a new beginning.

Archaeological evidence suggests a four-phase development of the Bigbury hilltop settlement/fort. First, in the Early Iron Age circa 450 B.C. as an undefended farmstead, abandoned, but resettled with a west-facing cross-ridge dyke towards the end of the Middle Iron Age period circa 200 B.C., when the story is set. The massive prestige hill-fort defences with dwellings and workplaces and a compound for cattle or slaves came into being in the first century B.C. Calyad and his story are fiction, but based on evidence of something having happened in East Kent in the Middle Iron Age, when, in contrast to earlier and later periods, there were very few settlements – or so it appears from the archaeological record. No one knows why this corner of Britain appears at this time to have been virtually deserted, hence the suggestion of pestilence. Elsewhere, defended hilltop forts had already become the norm; but here in East Kent we know only of Bigbury which was not to be fully-established until several generations later.

TALE FOUR

The Battle for Bigbury

Within five or six generations of the re-establishment of settlement on Bigbury, events were moving fast. The hilltop site had been enlarged and fortified with banks and ditches and an intricate eastern entrance. It was now a busy, bustling place, with iron, leather and pottery making, food stores, and was the probable home of the local tribal chief and his retinue. Traders came and went, bringing products from across the sea, including wine; slaves were passed on from the west to be sold across the Channel. Although still largely wooded, the high ramparts carved out of the hillside would have been an impressive sight, much their intention for conspicuous wealth and power was now the custom. The countryside around Harbledown would have been a patchwork of corn fields and paddocks for cattle and horses, with clusters of round farmhouses dotted about, smoke spiralling up into the sky. A network of trackways laced the homes and fields together, the forest was being pushed back but the Blean wood remained mainly intact, except for small iron-working clearings. The land was filling up, probably taking in refugees from across the sea who brought with them their distinctive 'Belgic' styles. There was a new force making itself felt across the narrow seas: the might of Rome . . .

Caesar sighed. It had been hard enough to get the fleet of eight hundred ships with their thirty thousand men, the horses and pack-animals across the Channel the night before last, keeping them all together, let alone landing, unloading and setting up camp. Still, his young officers and the seasoned Centurions had served him well whilst the hard core of his five legions had made the trip the year before. And that nearly ended in disaster, he reminded himself. At least, two legions knew what to expect from these Britons. Not that these folk are much different from their

Gallic cousins, the nobles amongst them given to squabbling, raiding each other for slaves and cattle, drinking heavily and bragging loudly.

Certainly, in recent years they had acquired a taste for some of the good things of Roman life, especially our wine. He smiled to himself.

"I wonder if they realised our merchant traders weren't just interested in their corn, their slaves and hunting dogs, their gold and silver but also their strong-held places – and their weaknesses. They have a certain proud conceit, these Britons, but then so had the Gauls – though they've been taught a sharp lesson. So too the Britons last year when we came, and saw, and conquered, albeit only for a short while. Perhaps that's why they didn't oppose our landing on that wretched exposed beach?"

He pushed aside the memory of his anxious thoughts as the first cohorts had waded ashore at midday the previous day. He had expected any moment a horde of darting two-wheeled chariots to charge across the open beach down on his men as they struggled to gain a footing. But nothing happened.

And now, by the Gods, he felt nervous again – and tired. Not surprising as he had taken his main force on an overnight march from the coast, inland twelve miles across the low wooded hills along an ancient trackway. It had been a slow, eerie trek, ill-lit by moonlight. They had arrived at dawn at the best shallow ford across the river, later to be known as the Great Stour.

From his spies and scouts, Caesar knew the main force of Britons was massing here, just downslope from one of their damned hill-forts, that one over there. By-passing the downstream deserted, spread-out collection of huts and enclosures overlooking the swampy river valley, his force had come to the river crossing. Sure enough, they were confronted by a milling mass of horsemen and chariots, streaming down from the wooded hillsides, shouting and screaming, waving swords and spears, war horns howling, drums thudding.

The legions locked firm, the Roman cavalry swept out in an iron phalanx and smashed through the swirling horde – again and again. The Britons broke off, turned and sped away, many to the great wooded hump of the hill-fort which rose above the valley. They were gone, but not without cost to Caesar's army. Well-aimed spears and slingshots had taken their toll and Caesar knew this kind of fighting, harrying hit-and-run tactics, with ambushes from the woods, could eventually wear down the most hardened and heavily-armed legionaries. They could only stand firm and take what was thrown at them. Cavalry was the answer – speed, determination, the iron fist.

"Meantime, we must take out this hill-fort," he thought. "And soon."

By the time the column had crossed the river it was already midday, the sun stood high in the sky and it was warm; but Caesar noticed away to the west great white clouds piling up in the sky. From what he knew of Gaul that could mean a midsummer storm approaching. Another stab of anxiety hit him. "I hope that fool Quintus Atrius remembers to get the boats beached."

He turned his mind to the task at hand. From the low hill on which he stood he could see the hill-fort's main eastern entrance, about fifteen hundred paces away. It had been blocked with felled trees. Although the wooded ridge looked formidable he judged the three ditches and banks which reared up and girdled its flanks were nothing like as daunting as those he had seen in Gaul. The gateway, as usual, was an interlocking series of banks, now crowded with shouting and howling Britons, warriors and women too, he noticed. Their roar of defiance echoed across to him. "Let them shout," he thought. "The more noise, the less energy when it comes to fighting."

Downslope from him his legions stood in solid phalanx, their lines arcing away to cover the flanks of the hill. His men were alert for any sudden foray from the woods around them. Even now, small groups of chariots and horsemen raced and leaped across the open fields, taunting the legionaries to break ranks and pursue. The toughened troops stood firm.

Caesar called the commander of the 7th Legion over. His instructions were precise and clear. Within minutes legionaries were hacking down small trees and bushes, tying them into bundles, collecting baskets of earth. The cavalry wheeled out to form a protective screen. Soon, all was ready. The 7th re-formed into a dense column, the five thousand or so men packed close, shields high, pilum spears at the ready.

A blast from the horn and slowly, with measured tread, the Legion marched, the sun glinting off its helmets and armour. Suddenly, all was quiet – except for the rhythmic thud of marching feet.

Caesar crossed his fingers behind his back and looked straight ahead, masking his excitement with a fixed stare. Slowly but relentlessly the 7th narrowed the gap. Closer and closer they came heading not for the gate but a little way off to one side.

Then the ramparts erupted. A great roar rose from the Britons. Some leapt down and charged, swords swinging, hurling themselves on the column. The Legion tramped on over their bodies without pausing.

An order rang out and the front of the column locked shields over their heads forming the time-honoured testudo or 'tortoise'. From above slingshot round pebbles buzzed through the air, spears, lumps of flint and chalk swished and thudded down. Men fell but the gaps were instantly filled. Forming a protective corridor, the legionaries took a heavy pounding but already the relays of bundled faggots and baskets of earth were being passed up the column and into the first ditch. It was hard, hot work. Soon the ground was slippery with blood, the air filled with the cries and groans of the wounded, the curses and grunts of the legionaries and the blood-curdling shouts of the defenders. Volleys of pilum and slingshots rose from the soldiers flanking the testudo – and many found their mark, the defenders pitching forward into the ditch.

Suddenly, across the face of the column, the first ditch was full – faggots, earth and bodies mixed together. The 7th surged up, over and on to the earth-bank. Now it was their turn. Out flashed the short gladius swords, deadly effective in close in-fighting. They jabbed and chopped methodically.

Within minutes the Britons had been swept off the bank and the legionaries had cleared the gateway of defenders. Leaping across the blocking tree-trunks the main force thundered into Bigbury. The Britons fled. The hill-fort was Caesar's. It had been just an hour since the 7th Legion marched forward. All that remained was to clear the vast, twenty-five acre, enclosed ridge-top, round up the pigs and cattle, see to the wounded legionaries, dispatch any wounded Britons, loot the scattered huts and question the handful of prisoners.

Caesar felt pleased, relieved but tired. He decided both he and his men deserved and had earned a rest. He called off pursuit of the beaten enemy – they were hot-footing away to the west. Time enough tomorrow.

He gave orders for the army to make camp and by late afternoon the rectangular one hundred and fifty acre "marching camp" had been established – a shallow-ditched and palisaded earth-bank within which all, except the guards, could get a good night's sleep, the first in three days.

Before he turned in, Caesar glanced westwards. The clouds were thickening, a strong breeze flapped his tent. Again the thought occurred to him:

"I hope that fool Quintus Atrius beached the boats."

30

This imagined account is based on Caesar's own version of his second expedition in force to Britain in early July, 54 B.C., written by him as much for self-glorification as straight history. Caesar's "marching camp" established after the battle for Bigbury is yet to be found – it is thought to be in the vicinity of Harbledown, perhaps near one of the streams.

Caesar's concern about his fleet was correct. On the night after Bigbury was taken, a great storm blew up, destroying forty ships which were anchored off-shore, with many others being severely damaged. Caesar had to return to the coast and spend ten valuable days reorganising his base. He then struck inland again, beat the Britons under their war-leader Cassivelaunus, made peace terms and returned to Gaul at the end of August. The Romans did not come again until A.D. 43. Those wasted ten days might have seen the Romans here to stay earlier – and history might have been different.

TALE FIVE

The Roman Way

After Caesar's assault on Bigbury it seems the hilltop was resettled for about a generation and then completely abandoned, the centre of activity shifting down to where Canterbury now stands. Here a sprawling settlement emerged, with a large central ditched enclosure. It was on this site, at the river-crossing where the main trackways (and later roads) from Dover, Folkestone, Lympne and especially Richborough met before heading on to London, that the Roman conquerors encouraged the building of a local administrative city. For the Romans, towns were the mark of civilised life – and their expression of power over a conquered land. It was through towns they ruled, collected taxes and brought into the Roman way the local native leaders. At this time, from the conquest in A.D. 43, Harbledown would have changed little except for the new road, a real road, which snaked up and over and around the local hills, bringing a continuous flow of people and goods. Along the road there may have been wayside temples, the occasional small villa-farm, often as not built by a local Briton keen to adopt the Roman fashion. Otherwise little altered, the local farmers still living in their traditional round huts, with small fields and paddocks, still hemmed in by the forest all around and with the deserted Bigbury looming on the skyline as a reminder of days now over . . .

The eleven-year-old twins, Aulus and Julia, paused on the brow of the hill and gazed out over the wide valley.

"Look, there, see!" said Julia, excitedly pointing towards the city. "See how it stands above all the other buildings. Do you think father will let us go down with him to get close to it again? It's grown so high."

"Maybe," replied Aulus, shrugging his shoulders. "If we catch him in the right mood."

33

The twins lived a short distance away, down the other side of the hill where the road from the city, Durovernum Cantiacorum or Canticor as they called it for short, crossed the small stream and bore off again uphill, regaining its direct straightness, heading for Londinium. Standing just off the road, their home was a small, oblong, timber-framed, four-roomed farmhouse with a verandah looking out south towards the old hill-fort. It was built to the Roman style with a red tiled roof and soon, if the harvests continued to be good, would have two wing-extensions added. Or so their father promised. And perhaps a small bath-house too? For the rest, there were a few outhouses and sheds, a herb garden and their fields, which ran gently downslope to the stream and up again towards the wooded hilltop. Rich soil meant good crops, whilst over the road began the thick forest, good for timber, pig grazing and deer hunting.

Aulus and Julia were the children of a local quite well-to-do landowner, a Briton who could trace his ancestry back over eight generations to before the Romans came and conquered. Family legend had it that one of their forebears had fought in the great battle against the venerated Caesar when he took the old hill-fort. Although now Romanised in many ways, in dress, eating habits, farming methods, these Romano-Britons still clung on to remnants of ancient local customs, worshipping their own gods, albeit with new names, marking the sun festivals, retaining much of their Celtic identity. The twins' father, Gitus, was wealthy enough to be required to undertake public duties down in the city, for many years now the administrative capital of this part of Kent. Once a sprawling collection of huts, fields and paddocks spread out along both banks of the marshy river, a real city had emerged but it was still unwalled. "Well, a city by its buildings and name, if not by its shape," their father observed. But then he had visited other places in his younger years.

Now, as the twins looked down across the fields towards the built-up area, they could pick out the two main roads, one off to the left which eventually led on to the great fort at Rutupiae, the other, more directly ahead, going straight on to the busy port of Dubris. Alongside and between these two parallel main highways was the oblong-shaped city, a grid of large and small townhouses, shops, craftsmen's workplaces and public buildings, but rising above them, clearly now, was the upper part of the new yet unfinished massive stone-built theatre. A shaft of sunlight caught it, white and shiny crisp through the pall of smoke rising from the kilns and iron-furnaces down towards the river.

It was the fifth year of the rule of Emperor Caracalla (A.D. 216), a young man who had ensured his inheritance from his father Septimus Severus, by having his own brother and joint-emperor Geta murdered – or so it was said. Severus had died at Eboracum after campaigning in the far northern lands. He left a good legacy with new forts and defences against the wild, untamed tribes north of the Wall. Caracalla had also made his mark first by dividing Britannia into two provinces and then just two years before, by issuing an edict conferring Roman citizenship on all free subjects of the empire, much to the delight of many, like the twins' father, who could now enjoy privileges long denied them. No longer "peregrini", "non-citizens", the ordinary Romano-Britons could claim the rights and protection of Roman law, rather than be judged by the old client ruling families, the descendants of those local chieftains who had quickly collaborated with the new Roman masters straight after the conquest. This was one of the reasons Durovernum was getting a new theatre, a gesture of thanks, suggested rather forcefully by the consular governor in Londinium. Emperor Caracalla, like his father Severus, was keen to celebrate his rule by outward and visible signs and in Durovernum the old theatre was small, out-dated and crumbling. This new theatre promised much. It was being built in the classical style, a huge D-shape, with banked seating for as many as seven thousand five hundred spectators, so folk could come from miles around on festival holy days and for celebrations of great events – and most, now, except for the slaves, as full citizens of the empire.

The twins turned for home. It was a hot, sultry midsummer evening and as they walked back over the crest of the hill Aulus suddenly noticed a long-robed, cowelled figure beckoning him. The strange, black-clad apparition had emerged from the path to the new holy place, the small, recently-built Mithras temple. It was set back from the road on the hill-crest, hidden and almost enclosed by trees. It was whispered it was almost all underground, a dark, strange place.

Aulus hesitated. His father had told him to keep clear of the temple and its priests, even though it was so close to home. It was muttered strange rites were performed there in the worship of a young Sun God, come from the east. Not that such worship was unknown to Aulus and his family. They celebrated the rebirth of the Sun at every winter solstice, watching its red disc sink behind the old hill-fort, praying for its return and building up great fires to drive back the dark. They would be out tonight, the night of midsummer, staying up until the next dawn, waiting, again with a huge fire so that there was no real darkness.

"Wait for me," said Aulus as he walked cautiously over to the hooded figure, fingering the knife in his belt as he went.

"Don't be afraid, young man." The voice was high and fluting, strange from such a stocky figure. The priest's eyes seemed to burn from beneath his cowl, boring into Aulus' frightened face.

"I want you to take a message to your father. Now he is a full citizen of the empire both he and you will be welcome to join us tonight, here at our temple. We can teach you much. No womenfolk, though. Go now, remember what I have said." With that the figure turned and disappeared into the bushes.

Aulus gulped, spun round and ran quickly to his sister and told her what had been said.

"A strange message, but why us, why me?" he asked.

Julia tossed her head. "Just like you men, always wanting to have silly secrets." They sped home, Aulus breathless with his message.

"I think not, my boy," said his father, looking worried and anxious. "This Mithras god attracts soldiers, fighting men, and travelling merchants from the other end of the empire. Strange men, some of them, with strange likings. We'll stay close to home tonight and leave such mysteries to those who wish them. We have our own old ones to celebrate. We know where we are with them. No need for us of any new-fangled young god out of the east. Anyway, they have taken one of our holy places from us. One day we shall have to reclaim it. But not tonight." With that, the subject was closed but to the twins' delight their father promised to take them down to the city the next day; partly, they agreed later, to take their minds off the strange encounter.

The next morning, still tired from the overnight midsummer vigil, the twins set off for the city. They followed the gravelled road downhill, across the fields, through the noisy, smoky industrial quarter to the wooden bridge over the river. Now they were amongst a busy, seething crowd – people and herds and flocks of farm animals, sheep, cattle, pigs, goats and geese, carts piled high with farm produce, others with tiles or blocks of stone, trains of pack-horses, some with baskets of oysters from the coast, freemen and women and slaves, with panniers on their backs full of chickens, ducks, vegetables and fruits. Children ducked and dodged through the crowds; the noise was deafening, the smells heavy in the warm, still air.

An Imperial messenger clattered by with his escort, heading for Londinium no doubt. He had probably stopped overnight at the fine, roadside mansio for a break on his journey up the road from Dubris. A small squad of Germanic auxiliaries tramped by, tall, blond-haired men with square, unsmiling faces. Here and there the twins saw finely dressed, dark-skinned merchants from the east.

They soon turned into a wide street off to the left, jammed with carts full of building stone, queuing to deliver their loads to the new theatre site. Already it reared up above them, swathed in scaffolding and with hoists hauling up great blocks of finished stone.

"Well, here it is," said their father proudly. "It should all be finished by the mid-winter festival. Truly a theatre worthy of our city."

The twins gaped for they had never before seen such a massive building. They had come close some months ago but now its sheer size took their breath away. To think they would be able to come here, sit in it and take part in the festivals and celebrations.

"We'd better move on," said their father. "I have some important things to do at the Basilica. Come with me to the Forum square and then I'll pay for you to be taken round the Temple precinct. But mind you behave with reverence."

They walked past the arched, beehive-shaped public baths, now busy with customers for it was a favourite meeting place to exchange news and gossip and do deals. This too was soon to be rebuilt. Turning left again, they joined the other wide road, the one which came in from Rutupiae. This was lined with large townhouses whose gardens were hidden behind high walls. The road was crowded and busy with through-traffic of all kinds but they soon came to the pillars leading into the huge Basilica, the local government offices and meeting place, Durovernum's main public building. It too was now beginning to show its age, having stood for well over a century. They passed through it out on to the wide expanse of the Forum, a great open space of hard-packed gravel, now swarming with people, market stalls and sellers, for this was the popular midsummer fair. Edging their way through the jostling crowd they came to the pillared entrance to the Temple complex. Here there was the usual assortment of poor folk and cripples, begging for alms.

The twins were entrusted to an elderly Temple attendant, a slight, grey-haired, kindly-faced man who was bidden to return them to the Basilica at midday. He took the twins into the precinct. Before them, in a wide, rectangular courtyard, stood a magnificent building, not big, but beautiful with its columns and ornate, coloured stonework. It had wide steps leading up into it.

"We cannot go in, but if we stand here we can hear the priests chanting. And smell the holy smoke," their elderly guide said.

Later, he took them round the wide, colonnaded walkway, cool on this hot summer's day. They gazed out across the courtyard, with its impressive fountain and scattering of small shrines and open-air altars, each with a group of worshippers clustered around.

"What's that there?" asked Julia, pointing to a small, square building in the corner of the precinct.

"That's ours, yours, mine," smiled their guide. "A shrine to our gods, the old ones who were here before the emperors came. They are a strange lot, these Romans. They have their own gods and make their emperors into gods but they don't mind us keeping ours, providing we give them Roman-sounding names."

Time slipped by and soon it was approaching midday. The twins met up with their father who took them to eat at one of the many food stalls.

"As this is a special day I will buy you each a present," he told them. So they wandered the busy streets, looking over the stalls and open-fronted shop displays until finally settling on a fine pair of silver earrings for Julia and a sturdy cloak-fastening for Aulus. Both were in the latest Roman style but had been made by a local craftsman, well known for his fine work.

By now the twins were thoroughly tired out – it had been a long, exciting night and a hot, exhausting day. Fortunately their father spotted a neighbour's ox-drawn cart heading out of the city, across the raised road over the marshy riverside to the other bridge. They hitched a lift, a slow, jolting ride which took them past the smoking kilns and ironworks, skirting the edge of the wide burial ground with its funeral pyres before turning sharp left, on past two or three farms before linking up with the Londinium road at the foot of their hill.

As the oxen heaved and grunted up over the hilltop Julia tugged Aulus' tunic. "Look, he's there again!"

Standing on the edge of the road was the dark-cowelled Mithras priest. He stood stock still but his burning eyes followed them as they passed by.

Aulus felt a chill of fear – and fascination – run through him. What was this strange new Roman way, he wondered. Why him?

He was to find out seven years later when as a young auxiliary officer serving at a fort far to the north on Hadrian's Wall he was initiated into the brotherhood of Mithras, part of the Roman way.

The family and incidents are obviously fiction but there is some archaeological evidence (Roman tiles, pottery) to suggest a small villa-farm on the site of Hopebourne. Likewise, St. Michael's church carries on its inside southern wall a stone carved with what appears to be the Mithraic sun god and two bulls fighting, said to have been part of the church fabric since at least A.D. 1250. Given its roadside, hilltop location it is quite possible there was a Mithraic temple here, not least as the church is dedicated to St. Michael, the slayer of devils, often imposed on pagan holy places to keep them suppressed. The evidence for the appearance and importance of Canterbury increases with every new excavation within the city and is now well documented.

TALE SIX

Herebeald's Dun

The four hundred years of Roman rule left only a slight imprint on Harbledown but much more so for Canterbury where the city flourished before sliding into ruin and almost total abandonment. As the Empire began to crack and crumble both from within and without, the city itself began slowly but perceptibly to disintegrate. At the end of the third century A.D. it contracted behind defensive walls and, as the threat from sea-going Saxon raiders increased and rebellion and revolt within the Province and Empire recurred, it began to falter, reviving temporarily from time to time, but inevitably falling into disrepair and ruin.

Around 412 A.D. the last legions pulled out, leaving the Britons to fend for themselves and squabble over territory and religion. The city was further abandoned, finally collapsing into urban decay. Out in the countryside the way of life went on but fear and famine drove people away westwards, though some remained. At Harbledown it is likely a few British farms survived, not least because the old road remained. But now those staying on had to be self-sufficient, no longer able to go down to the city for trade and enjoyment. And a different people were moving in from across the sea, the Jutes. The old hill stood waiting for a new owner, one of the incomers . . .

Herebeald paused at the crumbling city gate, sniffing the air. "This place smells old and stale and sour," he thought, scratching his beard. He had been walking half the morning, setting out at dawn from the coastal village where he had landed two days before. He was glad to have the chance to stretch his legs after the full-five-days' sea-journey from his homeland in a cramped, well-laden, ten-oared, open boat. He had come to make a new life in this old land. They had sailed south, hugging the low coastlands, then with a hard haul across the narrow seas had turned

41

up the wide salt-water estuary to a river mouth where they landed. Here he met his uncle, AElaff, the one who had sent for him with promises of a good life and rich land to farm.

AElaff had made the same journey himself some six years before, part of the hired warrior-band who had come over the seas to fight for the Briton chief, Vortigern. But they had been cheated, so took land for themselves as recompense, including the island the Britons called Tanatus, over the channel from AElaff's homestead. AElaff had not prospered as much as his message suggested. Even now he was racked with marsh-fever, coughing and spluttering as he spoke. Herebeald took little time to leave this dark, misty marshside place and head inland, up the valley, following the straight Roman road, now rutted and pitted with grass and weeds taking hold.

He passed isolated, mainly deserted farms, there were few people in sight and many of the fields were untended. He came to a ford and picked up the line of the road across the other side, leading him to the place where the old city still stood. His uncle had told him some of their own folk had settled there, but it was a strange, deserted place.

He stood at the wrecked city gate, broken and falling down, as were the high stone walls off to each side. Herebeald had heard of such places, of how the people lived like the Romans even though they weren't really Romans, how they had copied their customs, their dress, even their gods, including this Christ he kept hearing about, the god they had killed. What puzzled him was the idea of choosing to live crammed together behind high walls in what they called cities. Strange folk these.

That was all now finished. The end had begun slowly, many generations ago when his own forebears, the Jutes and other neighbouring seafarers started raiding across the seas, lured by wealth and goaded by poor harvests. Some war-bands had been recruited as Roman auxiliaries to guard the coast against their own kin. A strange idea, Herebeald thought. Even stranger, the Roman Britons let them bring over their families and gave them land to settle on. And now their fine way of life had collapsed, well here, at least. Once the Roman armies finally left a generation before, the British chief-men had begun to fight amongst themselves. Now *that* Herebeald could understand.

Although he was only twenty years old Herebeald already knew much, by word of mouth, of what had happened. Traders, raiders, mercenaries plied back and forth across the seas and knowledge of events travelled with them. So when his uncle sent word, he came. His own home village was poor, the soil thin and sandy, the sea was forever flooding in across the salt-marshes – and there were too many mouths to feed. He had packed his few possessions in a leather back-pack, sharpened his spear, checked his bow, made his farewells and left, volunteering as an oarsman for the sea-passage.

It was early spring in the year known as A.D. 455, a time of change, of old endings and new beginnings. "And this city place is surely ending," thought Herebeald.

It was strangely quiet. He had noticed as he approached the gateway there was no birdsong, something which made him feel uneasy. "The sign of a dead place," he thought. Hitching up his pack and grasping his spear haft firmly, he strode into the town. The road underfoot was worn and rutted, with grass and weeds springing up. To either side there were buildings, some still standing whole but with sagging upper storeys and broken columns. Others were roofless or with collapsed walls, with their tiles, masonry and burnt or rotting timbers tumbled across parts of the roadway. Here and there what had been walled gardens, burst out with young trees, bushes and shrubs spreading over heaps of rubble, invading open plots of land. Picking his way gingerly through the foul-smelling undrained pools and thick, sticky patches of mud, silt and mire, he walked on. Then, ahead, he saw a huge ruin looming up, covered with small trees and bushes growing out of every crack and crevice.

His uncle had told him to head for this, the centre of the city, for it had once been the meeting place of the Britons, a theatrum they called it. Close by he would find some of his own folk who had chosen to set up home in this strange place. There were even a few Britons lurking about in the ruins but these were poor dispossessed people, old and likely mad. Sure enough he could smell smoke, hear voices, even the sound of cattle, sheep and geese. He soon came across a cluster of long-huts, some butted up against existing walls, others standing free with small gardens. Close by he noticed a wide open grassy expanse, littered with stone column-stumps and blocks. A group of children came running to greet him, inquisitive, keen to know where he came from, would he stay, where was he going?

He was formally welcomed by the headman of this village in the city, a cheery, straight-backed man who himself had come over with AElaff. Herebeald was fed and rested as was the custom and in turn explained his journey. But he needed to know more of this place so would they answer his questions? They courteously agreed. "Yes, it was an eerie place to live in but there was no shortage of usable building materials. Yes, the water was good but the part of the city down by the river often flooded so it was avoided except for cattle-grazing. It was a bad place to live, down there, dank and fever-ridden. No, there were very few Britons hereabout, they had mostly run away or moved out into the countryside, although some of the wives here are of British stock. Yes, there are a few traders passing through, mainly to cross the river. Yes, there are ghosts but yes, you are welcome to stay."

That night Herebeald slept uneasily. For all the warm welcome he did not feel at home. The weight of this dead city seemed to push in on him with its creaking ruins, its smell of death and decay, its wind mournfully howling round the tumbled stone walls. Surely the ghosts of generations roamed this place?

The next morning he made his thanks and farewells and left through another crumbling gateway, across a sagging wooden bridge, following an old, straight road through scrubby wasteland. He had not gone far when the road began to rise up towards a wooded hilltop. Reaching the crest he turned and looked back. There below him the line of the road ran across the neglected fields to the city, now bathed in a silvery early morning mist which blurred its outline, softened its jagged ruins. It looked better from up here, he thought. And suddenly he felt free, free of the dead city, free of the night fears.

It was then that he heard a cry – a wail of despair, there, over to his left, upslope, coming from within the dense mass of trees which pressed to the road's edge. Hefting his spear he broke into a loping trot towards the sound, now of loud sobs. There was an overgrown track. Stealthily, advancing slowly, he pushed through the tangled undergrowth and came to a clearing. Ahead, on the ground, a pale-faced, distraught young woman knelt, cradling an elderly and clearly dead man in her arms. Close by stood two young children, a small boy and an older girl, their arms round each other, crying bitterly.

Herebeald halted, resting his spear-point down to the ground, a sign of peaceful intent. The children spotted him first and ran to the young woman with fear on their faces. The three of them crouched, huddled together, now silent and apprehensive. For a few moments Herebeald was at a loss what to do. Obviously, from the way they were dressed, their dark-brown hair, the way they clung to each other, these must be local folk, Britons. And Death had been a recent visitor. He glanced around. There was no sign of a struggle, no blood. He relaxed. The only sound was birdsong, high in the trees around the clearing. That was a good omen.

Herebeald lifted his spear and drove it firmly into the soft earth. He then extended both hands, palms outwards to show he carried no other weapon. Slipping his pack off he sat down cross-legged, to indicate he was not going to leap upon them – and he tried to smile reassuringly. They stayed like this, staring at each other, each waiting for the other to move or speak.

Finally, the young woman said something, but Herebeald shook his head, not understanding. Then he had an idea. Reaching back into his pack he pulled out the half of round loaf given to him that morning when he left the city settlement. Holding it out, he beckoned to them. There was no response, so he gently threw it across the grass to them. The small boy eagerly grabbed it up – and they gave a half-smile of thanks to him. The young woman, something of a beauty Herebeald noticed for the first time, held out her hands, copying his peace greeting.

He stood up, but stayed still. The young woman also got to her feet. Casting around for the few words of the British language he had picked up from traders, Herebeald struggled to explain who he was, where he had come from, what he was doing here. The young woman suddenly laughed and began to tell him, in his own language but in a strange dialect, that she understood him. It transpired later she had learned the words from an old farmhand who had worked her father's land, a Saxon who had before that served as an auxiliary, one who had hired his sword to the British rulers but had never returned to his homeland. Her name was Selena, she explained, and these were her sister and brother, Drusa and Vix. The dead man was their father who had, with no warning, dropped and died whilst out with them. They were now all alone, as their mother had died the previous year of a raging fever and the farmhands had all fled west months ago. Until a few years back they had lived down in the old city but had moved out here to the family farm, for safety and health. Life had been hard, trying to work the small remaining vegetable plots, keeping the two cows and the few chickens. Her father was a good man but not used to labouring, and his previous wealth and power now counted for nothing. But what were they to do? They had, so they thought, an uncle in Londinium but that was, by all accounts, a dangerous trek to make. So they would stay and make the best of what they had. Her grief, anguish and uncertainty poured out, but in a controlled and practical way, thinking not just of the now, but of things to come.

Herebeald was impressed. Here was a young woman of courage and determination but he doubted if even she could make a life here on her own for herself and the two youngsters. He offered his help, first to bury their dead father, which they did, in the clearing where he had died.

Later, having been taken back to the dilapidated, run-down farmhouse to eat, sit and talk further, Herebeald struck a bargain with Selena. He would stay and help with the farmwork until the autumn. He had already reckoned this was a good place, well-sheltered and watered, with rich soils, plenty of timber to hand and opportunity for hunting in the woods. A good way to get used to this new land. It also seemed a healthy spot, here, high on the hill, away from that stinking ghost town.

So he stayed, through to the autumn and the next. He never left, taking Selena, with her consent, as his wife and partner, fathering a family of his own. The hilltop farm became known as "Herebeald's Dun" – and in this way he is still with us.

The exact origins of the name Harbledown are uncertain, although Herebeald's Dun is one favoured option. There is a suggestion that Harble equates to Herbal, linking the name to the arrival of the Norman leper hospital and its herb garden. If so, why not Lepers' dun or hill? The suffix 'dun' is the Old English and more likely Celtic for 'hill' and suggests a pre-Norman settlement with a pre-Norman name. Archaeological evidence indicates Romano-British Canterbury was well into decline and ruin by the mid-5th century but with Jutish settlers already squatting in the decayed city with perhaps no total abandonment within the walls. Evidence also suggests early Saxon/Jutish incomers arrived not as waves of conquerors but rather over a long period as individuals or in family groups, boat people who likely intermarried with the local Britons, merging into the landscape, bringing new fashions, new customs, a new language. This was a cultural rather than a racial takeover.

TALE SEVEN

The Christman Cometh

Christianity was not new to Britain when Augustine arrived on his mission from Pope Gregory in A.D. 597. Under Roman rule Christianity had at times been subject to persecution but mostly was tolerated as just another imported eastern cult, finally becoming the official Imperial choice under Constantine the Great in A.D. 313. Even so, many Celtic religious customs and festivals continued and the influx of Jutish and Saxon newcomers before and after the Roman withdrawal brought a further variety of Pagan belief and ritual.

At the time of Augustine's arrival a strong and wealthy Kingdom of Kent had emerged, with powerful alliances with the Frankish lands across the Channel. Trade flourished, as did the manufacture of fine jewellery and weapons. Canterbury was beginning to re-emerge as a recognisable market town or burh, the countryside was dotted with farms and hamlets, the forests were being pushed back. Harbledown would have shared in this expansion, not least because of its association with the old street or road, its nearness to Canterbury and its rich soils. By now the field-pattern would have changed, long strips up and down the gentle slopes, with hedges and trackways. The forests still pressed in, a valuable resource not least for hunting. The people practiced their old religion but that was soon to change – or was it?

Peter the monk plodded out of the city, if you could call it that. He was not a happy man. A thin drizzle falling from low, grey clouds misting in from the north coast on a chilly wind added to his downcast spirits. Could it only be just two years since he had left Rome with his thirty-nine companions to accompany the holy abbot Augustine, sent by Pope Gregory to bring God's word to these Saxon or Jute or whatever they call these heathen folk? It felt more like a lifetime since leaving those softer,

47

warmer lands where life was easier, even for a monk. At least it was warm and dry in the old monastery, not cold and wet most of the year like this accursed place.

It had been bad enough crossing the narrow seas early in the year, pitching and tossing in the narrow boat but then, once they had landed, there was that long walk across the island, Tantus was it called? To add further insult they then had to endure the indignity of waiting on a windswept hillside for this so-called King AEthelbert to arrive. A meeting in the open air all because the King was afraid of the Abbot's magic. Magic indeed! King indeed! If it wasn't for the fact AEthelbert had married Bertha, daughter of the Christian Frank King Charibert, we wouldn't be here. But she had brought over that simpleton Frankish bishop Liuhard who couldn't leave well alone. So here we are, and a miserable place it is.

Peter picked his way carefully along the muddy, mirey, dung-spattered road out of Cantawaraburh. It was early spring in the year A.D. 598. Since arriving in the town Peter and his companions had been hard at work with some of the King's slaves, beginning to build their own abbey church. This was on some land AEthelbert had given them just outside the town's tumbled walls, not far from the old, part-restored Christian church used by Queen Bertha. Meantime they had been forced to live like the locals, in primitive timber, wattle and thatched long-huts with sunken earth floors, lacking any real comfort and warmth. The King, when he was staying in Cantawaraburh, lived in a royal hall, well defended on two sides by the patched-up old walls and a stout palisade for the rest. He had other halls scattered at key points across his lands and moved between them, keeping a firm grip on his subjects and on the wealthy traders passing through.

As for Cantawaraburh itself, Peter had nothing but contempt. In his eyes it was not a town but a sprawling, shapeless village of tracks, primitive farm huts interspersed with patches of grazing land, small vegetable gardens, with scattered trees and bushes growing on the hummocky ruins of what had probably been fine buildings. The remains of what was once a tall, stone construction, a theatre perhaps, stood high over the surrounding huts. Here and there the stumps of columns poked through the undergrowth. The town walls were crumbling into the surrounding ditch but in places had been strengthened with wooden palisades. The gates were a disgrace and down by the river a large extent was now flooded and marshy. And inside the old walls at that. There was no drainage, and filth and refuse bogged the tracks. The people seemed cheerful enough though, going about their tasks, setting up stalls, making and selling iron goods, cloth, leather, even some fine-wrought silver and gold ware. But they were uncouth, coarse, smelly and loud-mouthed. Or so Peter thought. He had managed to master enough of their barbaric tongue to make himself understood but he still felt ill at ease when amongst them. In turn, he was treated with curiosity and a sort of indifferent respect. He and his companions were the King's guests; the King had taken to their god, the Christ. Those who wished to keep favour with the King were undergoing this baptism, they called it. If it pleased the King – or more likely the Queen – then so be it. It was generally accepted AEthelbert was so besotted with his Bertha that he would do almost anything to please her. And now she wanted new churches established out in the villages, with more souls saved.

So it was that Peter now made his way to Hereabald's doun, not far from his companions but for him it felt like exile. He had been chosen for this task not for any outstanding sign of devotion or willingness but, as the abbot had said, to curb his pride. "You will never be happy in this land until you see these people as God's creatures, not inferior beings. Since we came here you have done nothing but grumble and complain. Now go and live amongst them, take God's word to them but also learn from them."

These were not the only orders given him by the abbot Augustine. He was to respect the customs and ways of these people, seek out one of their holy places to build a church, bring them to God and Christ by example and persuasion. He was also to look out for any likely boys to send down to the abbey church for training. Peter warmed to this last command. "The sooner these people have their own priests, the sooner I'll be able to leave this land," he thought. But kept the thought to himself.

On he plodded, across the scruffy, open fields, heading for the hill. The old Roman road was still in use but after two centuries of neglect grass and weeds, even small trees and bushes, had encroached. There were potholes and patches of thick mud, it was more of a country track than an imperial highway. Still, it was busy, with cattle, sheep, pigs and geese being driven towards the town, well-laden pack-horses and mounted fine-folk travelling on their way west.

As Peter began toiling uphill there was a sudden commotion ahead of him. Over the crest came a stampeding herd of swine with a gangly youth in pursuit. Instinctively, Peter, who stood right in their path, raised his arms and cried out loudly three times, "Sui abiti!", "Swine go away!" The coarse-haired mob of pigs were so startled by this strange, black-clad apparition shouting at them that they swerved aside, squealing and panicking, to crash through a low hedge into a small enclosure. The youth quickly rounded them up and calmed them down. Peter watched with mixed feelings, part fright and part smug satisfaction. "Well," he thought, "at least the pigs understand the word of authority so maybe these brute folk will also do so. There's hope after all."

The youth, looking impressed, waved his thanks, and Peter continued his tiresome journey.

He was to seek out the local headman, a freeman or ceorl called Aelric. The King had already sent word ahead that he should make Peter welcome, give him due respect and get the other local folk to help build him both a home-house and a small place in which to worship. The site he left Aelric to decide upon. Down over the hill by a stream Peter came to a well-built farm-house, well-built by what he judged to be the standards of these Jutes. For him it appeared no more than a larger version of what he had seen in the ruined city, but well defined by hedge and fencing. A solidly-built man, dressed plainly but decently, stood waiting, grim-faced. Presumably this was Aelric. He grudgingly extended both hands to Peter, who in turn graciously nodded and made the sign of the cross. They stood looking at each other, neither sure what to do next. Suddenly the swineherd Peter had met earlier appeared and started talking rapidly, gesticulating at Peter. After a short while Aelric grinned, stepped forward and took Peter's arm, gesturing him to enter his home.

Sometime later Peter, by now warmed through, dry and feeling well-fed for the first time in months, managed to piece together the reason for Aelric's sudden change of expression from sullen unease to welcoming joviality. Apparently they thought he had used magic words to cause the runaway swine to bolt into the enclosure. Anyone with such useful knowledge and power was welcome – and respected. "Yes, it was magic, Christ's magic," Peter attempted to explain. "Christ took care of his own." This was received with some scepticism, for the assembled locals, by now crowding into Aelric's house, knew only too well how these Christians bled and died the same as any others, sometimes with less courage and fortitude than the true-folk. "But it was a start," Peter thought.

Over the next weeks, as the raw spring edged into summer, Peter found himself busier than he had been since he was a novice. Aelric chose for him a site on the hill-crest, overlooking Cantawaraburh, explaining it was an old holy place. Here, with the help of the villagers Peter soon had his own small hut and a herb garden. One day, whilst clearing back the undergrowth on the hilltop he came across what appeared to be the sealed-up entrance to an underground chamber. It looked suspiciously like the way down to one of those accursed Mithras-cult rooms he had been warned about, but he made no comment. He did, however, notice that the locals made strange signs whenever they came near it, as if to ward off evil spirits. He also observed that when they celebrated their own pagan festivals like the midsummer night, they went to another nearby hilltop to build their great all-night fires. Still, this site had its advantages, including giving him the opportunity to observe the comings and goings up the old road. He was also within easy walking distance of his holy brethren, though as time went on he found the need to visit them less and less appealing. He decided to build his church, a small, wooden construction, right over what he thought was the Mithras place. "Christ is strong enough to prevail against any heathen spirits lurking down below," he thought. He also calculated that it would impress the locals with Christ's strength.

So, when autumn came, Peter was established. By now he was able to converse reasonably well in the Jutish tongue and had already persuaded Aelric and his family to listen to the word of God, not always easy because these folk would keep asking searching questions, trying to make comparisons with their own gods and practices. More than once Peter had to bite his tongue to stop himself condemning their pagan ideas. But he also found his attitude towards them mellowing as he came to understand better their ways, not least their generosity towards him. In part, this was due to his skill with herbs and medicines, which some saw as more Christ magic. These folk were much given to believing in ghosts and spirit-forces, superstitions and charms but respected the healer above all. Peter thought he was gradually winning them round, or were they just being polite to him and doing as their King required? He had not made many outright converts but at least he was here, he had ample food, was treated with respect and was able to keep warm. In addition Aelric had made over to him an assistant, the young swineherd, Aelfgang, who, despite his awkwardness turned out to have a quick mind and a good memory. Perhaps he might make a novice? Peter began to teach him Latin and got him to help when he held services in his tiny church.

Augustine himself had come up from the abbey compound to bless and dedicate the church. Now that had been a great day. Queen Bertha and her retinue had come as well. She had showered the assembled villagers and those who had come in from outlying farms with gifts "for your Godliness," she told them.

"Godly they may be, but they still practice their pagan rites," thought Peter to himself. Not that all these heathen festivals were to his dislike. He felt this particularly when he was invited to share the feasting at Aelric's home at what they called Yule-tide, marking the shortest day of the year and the rebirth of the sun. Peter was well fed on pork, deer meat and goose and quickly developed a taste for the strong-brewed ale, joining in the toast, made over and over, of "Waes Hael!", "Be well!" He was sure Christ would approve and, after all, the holy Augustine had ordered him to respect their traditions. So be it.

Peter lived on at Hereabald's doun, never returning to Rome, but finding instead a love for these Jutish villagers, sharing with them their lives, joys and tribulations. He made converts, Aelfgang became a novice priest. Peter died at the ripe old age of fifty-five, a respected member of the local community. But in spite of all he said about them, which was not much, the local folk whilst now nominally Christian still insisted on celebrating, and that was the word, their old pagan festivals. After all, as they saw it, the Christman had come, but who knew, one day he might go away and the old gods return in the King's favour?

The Harbledown characters and situations are all fiction but the coming of Augustine, the conversion of King AEthelbert and the spread of nominal Christianity is documented. Nominal because pagan practices continued on, some of them down to the present day but subsumed by the Christian church. Archaeological evidence and early records indicate early Saxon churches were often sited on Romano-British and older holy sites, hence the suggestion there was an early precursor church beneath the Norman-built St. Michael's. Perhaps one day we shall find out.

TALE EIGHT

The Dane Dawn

During the four centuries between the arrival of Augustine and the Norman Conquest, the English kingdom consolidated and took on its own identity as a nation. But it was no easy task. Christianity took root and Canterbury became much more of an urban centre with its walls strengthened, its streets and houses close-packed. The cathedral arose, although not as we know it, along with a range of ecclesiastical buildings. Trade and industry flourished. However, the city's wealth attracted a new menace, the Danish Vikings. They came, pillaged and slaughtered in A.D. 842 and again in A.D. 852. The city survived, but the threat revived in A.D. 991 and continued for the next eleven years. The surrounding countryside, including Harbledown, was well farmed and villages and hamlets had emerged, rich and easy pickings for the marauding raiders . . .

Elfrida scooped up her baby son and ran out of the cottage, following the narrow path up into the woods. The sound of the war-horn warning echoed round the hills. The Danes, the Vikings, were coming again, just as they had two years ago and almost every year she could remember since her childhood. Now twenty-four, married with three children, a son of ten, a daughter of eight and a new baby girl, she lived with her freeman farmer husband Aelthan in a small but snug earthen-floored house, tucked into a fold in the hillside, here at Herebald's doun. She headed uphill to the gathering place, anxious her son and daughter would be there before her as she had earlier that late September morning sent them into the woods to collect nuts.

It was the year A.D. 1011 and the scourge of the raiding Danemen seemed to be getting worse. Now a great host, led by one Thorkell the Tall, had not only come to the English land but had stayed. And this was no ordinary war-host, by all accounts, but included fierce fighters from somewhere called Jomsborg, way across the wide sea, mad, crazed men who fought as if possessed by devils. For two years these invaders had ravaged the land, though fortunately the merchants and priests of Cantawaraburh and East Kent had bought them off when they first landed. Dane-geld they called it. Satisfied at wealth without war, the Danes had ridden back to their longships which they had left pulled up on-shore at Sandwicke. They then took themselves off to ravage the east Angles and Mercia. But now they were back, as always soon after the harvest had been gathered in. As Aelthan put it: "We work, they steal."

Elfrida reached the clearing, a well-sheltered, small, open meadow in the thick woods. She was relieved to see young Wulf and Matilda there. Other folk joined them, the men hastily armed with sword, axe or spear, some with their bows, others with whatever farm implement would serve as a weapon. The priest was there, a frail, wise old man who had seen and suffered much – but he was one of their own and was held in great respect. Soon it seemed as if the whole population of the scattered village and outlying farms was assembled, except for the three young lads who had gone, as was their task, to spy out the old road up from Cantawaraburh where it dipped down over the hill. From here they could see any who came from either direction.

Bitter experience over many generations had taught these people it was pointless to stand and fight in the open whilst few in number especially as the Danes had learned the value of horses. They rode and ravaged the land, fighting on foot with their fearsome war axes only when it suited them. The English King, AEthelred, seemed unable to bring together a good-sized war-host to expel the intruders whilst the rich merchants and churchmen, so it appeared, were able to buy peace, although increasingly at any price asked of them. For the common folk there was no protection, no wealth to spare, only themselves to rely on. Out of self-preservation they had made plans for what to do.

First, get up into the woods well away from the road to the place where they had hidden food and water and built secret shelters, at the same time setting a watch. Skilfully-made barriers of thorn and bramble blocked the narrow and almost indistinct pathway and circled the clearing, not least to keep out predatory foxes and other nosey woodland beasts. The next part was the hardest – the waiting. Was this just a speedy raiding party, seeking horses and food, or something worse, a thorough ravaging, with looting, burning, massacre and slave-taking?

It was a long wait but fortunately it was a crisp, fresh early autumn day with the sun bright and scattered white clouds piling high in a pale blue sky. Elfrida set Matilda to watch over the baby and went over to where the men and older wives were standing, quietly chatting. Because of his sword skill and good sense Aelthan had been chosen as leader for such a situation, with the much-travelled, wise old priest to give advice. It was said he had been a warrior in his younger days before taking holy vows. But he never spoke of this and when asked he just smiled and changed the subject. He had lived amongst them for many years, tending the tiny stone and timber chapel on the hilltop, turning a blind-eye when they celebrated the old pre-Christian seasonal festivals. He did his best to intercede for them at the ever-growing dues demanded by the churchmen down in the city who owned the land they farmed.

"The more they pay the Danes to be left alone, the more they ask of you and the more they leave you to fend for yourselves. This cannot be right," he had told them. "We must learn to stand together and seek our own salvation." So they did, with the women learning how to handle a spear and the small sceax sword.

Aelthan and the others were discussing how best to round up the livestock, the cattle, horses and pigs they had left out in the fields, pens and paddocks. "If they don't come soon, we'll have to chance it and bring them up into the woods. Crossing the old road will be the most dangerous time. Perhaps just a few to start with, the horses. It will be the horses they will want above all else." The others nodded their agreement.

It was then they heard the bird-call signal, repeated three times, telling them one of the lookout lads was coming in. Panting from his uphill run the boy told them he had seen smoke rising down-river from the city.

"So they have come up the channel in their boats again," said the priest. "That surprises me for there was word the Dane host now moved overland on horse. They must have resumed their old ways. I wonder where they landed?"

As the day wore on, the lookouts reported straggles of townsfolk fleeing the city, heading out along the old road. Also smoke from burning homesteads was getting nearer, now their side of the river and close to the city. Aelthan took two men and hid in the thick bushes at the roadside, hoping to stop one of the refugees to find out what was happening. They watched a small group reach the foot of the hill but to their horror saw a band of twenty or so armed horsemen galloping hard across the fields, yelling and whooping as they came. The riders caught up with the scattering group. The sun glinted on rising and falling swords and axes. It was quickly over. The raiders took little time to strip the bodies although there was a brief brawl over one of the pack-horses, soon resolved by the band's leader, a big burly man, who clipped one of the squabblers with his axe butt, knocking him flat on his back. The rest guffawed. The leader then pointed uphill, shouting orders. Four riders detached themselves from the war-band and started up the road, but slowly, reluctantly. The rest rode off towards Cantawaraburh, laughing and jeering.

Aelthan quickly sent one of his men back to fetch six others. They might be able to lure these Danes into the woods and send them to their warrior heaven. Meanwhile he would have to think of some way of delaying them, not that they seemed anxious to ride on, scouting through these thick wooded parts. He suddenly remembered the two mares and the foal left grazing in the paddock close by the chapel. They would be good bait. He told his companion to go to meet the others and bring them to the paddock but to await his signal.

He got up, leaving his sword hidden in the bushes, and walked out to the middle of the road, fully visible to the riders. He stood, arms folded, as the four Danish warriors approached. They were chunky men, broad-shouldered, riding their horses sloppily. Aelthan could see they were well armed, two with spears but also war axes dangling from their saddles. The other two carried swords. They saw him and stopped, puzzled by this strange, unarmed Englishman who barred their path. Clearly suspicious, they talked amongst themselves, wondering if this was some kind of trap. Aelthan extended his arms, showing his hands were empty and called out, "Horses?", as close to Dane-speak as he could. The oldest Dane, a greybeard wearing a battered helmet, waved back. "Yes, yes, horses."

Aelthan beckoned them to follow. Fortunately for him one of the mares decided to whinny loudly as if to confirm his offer. The bait was taken. Walking slowly, limping as if he had an injured leg, Aelthan led the four horsemen up the narrow lane, hoping his companions had made good speed. The Danes were still wary and followed some paces behind him. Round a thick hedge, there was the paddock, with the two mares and the foal, frisking in the autumn sunshine. Aelthan opened the gate and stood to one side, but back, out of spear reach. The Danes, now excited at the sight of the three fine animals, forgot their caution and cantered in, their eyes gleaming. "Greed often overcomes caution," the old priest had said. And so it was. They were so entranced they didn't notice when Aelthan quietly closed the gate behind them. The trap was sprung, or so he hoped. The sound of a magpie, sha-sha-sha-shak echoed across the paddock. All was ready.

Two of the Danes dismounted to walk over to the mares who, inquisitive as ever, trotted towards them. The other two raiders relaxed in their saddles, watching.

Now was the time to strike. Aelthan was about to give the signal to attack when, to his amazement, Elfrida stepped out of the trees, holding a spear. What was this? His mind raced, then it came to him what she was doing. The two mounted Danes slid out of their saddles, broad grins on their faces. They thought this was going to be good sport, no need for spears or axes to overpower this handsome-looking woman. They left their horses and weapons and began to walk slowly towards Elfrida, who still stood close to the tree edge, her spear held two-handed defiantly before her, glaring at the Danes with scorn. Now all four raiders approached her, the other two putting their weapons to one side for they reckoned they could take this woman with their bare hands.

Aelthan looked around for something to use and picked up a stout staff left propped against the fence. "This will do," he thought.

The Danes formed a half-circle around Elfrida jeering and taunting her, but keeping just out of spear-reach. They were totally caught up in their lust to inflict terror and their domination over this woman who dared to challenge them.

Aelthan started to run at them, shouting loudly to distract them, swinging his staff round his head. They turned to face him and as they did so the Hereabald's doun men leapt out of the bushes on to them. Elfrida lunged with her spear and caught one Dane deep in the side. Two others were beaten to the ground by the weight of numbers and speedily hacked and stabbed to death. The last raider, quicker than his companions, started to run towards his horse but Aelthan was upon him, giving him a mighty crack across the head, denting his helmet and dropping him to his knees. Aelthan butt-ended him on to his back and stood astride the outstretched, stunned Dane, the thick end of the staff pressing into his throat.

The villagers came running over, blood-lust in their eyes, clearly intent on finishing this one off. But Aelthan shouted to them to hold-fast. "We keep this one for now. Maybe he will tell us what their intentions are," he told them.

Elfrida came over to her husband, pale-faced but with a satisfied smile. She had proved for all to see that Englishwomen were brave, resourceful and could use their wits. Aelthan was both proud of her and bemused for women weren't meant to act like this – or perhaps they were?

The prisoner was tied up, the bodies stripped of everything useful and buried deep in the undergrowth. The horses were led away into hiding. By now dark-based thunder clouds were piling high into the afternoon sky. The old priest sniffed the air. "With God's good grace we shall soon have a storm to wash away the blood. The Danes will be sure to come looking for their lost men." Soon after a heavy downpour swept across the hilltops, cleansing the trampled earth.

Back at the refuge the prisoner soon came round and was taken out of ear-shot to be questioned by the priest and three others. At first he was stubborn, but the old priest, to the wry amusement of his assistants, turned out to be very skilled with a long, thin-bladed knife and soon the Dane was babbling. They had come to take all the wealth of Cantawaraburh but had found the city gates closed and the walls lined with armed men. The Dane host would now likely besiege the city although he could only guess at this as he and the rest of his band had been sent to catch those who were fleeing. The blood-spattered prisoner sobbed for mercy but the priest sent the villagers away and speedily finished him off, offering up a prayer as he did so.

Back in the hidden clearing the villagers felt mighty pleased with themselves but it was joy edged with fear. If the Danes were to lay siege to the city then they would be scouring the surrounding countryside for food and women. It could be a long wait, up here in the woods, with the need to remain ever vigilant and prepared. The old priest told them, "Archbishop Aelfheah is a stubborn man, as I well know. If he has decided to hold the city, and the men of Cantawaraburh follow him, then God save them all. And us. I pray he keeps a close watch on Abbot Aelfmaer, a scheming, treacherous man if ever there was. He is one who always, so I've been told, wants to make deals with the Danes. And you all know, to your cost, what that means."

It was twenty long days later when the whole village crept to the edge of the woods, near their chapel high on the hill, to look down over Cantawaraburh. For twenty days the city had been besieged, but now it was over. The night before they had watched with mounting fascination and horror as the city and great church burned. Somehow the Danes had managed to break in and had torched the town. All night the sky had glowed red, the glare of the flames reflecting back from low, sullen clouds. Now it was dawn, the fires had died down, but a thick pall of smoke hung over the misty valley.

One other strange thing had happened during that night. For days no one, other than scavenging groups of Danes, stopping off occasionally to torch a farmstead, had passed along the road. But towards dawn a small party of men, muffled but looking like priests, had gone by galloping hard up the hill.

"I wonder if that traitorous Aelfmaer was amongst them," mused the priest as the villagers knelt to pray for their kinsfolk in the city. "But look!" he ordered. "See the sun rising. See how it shows blood red through the black smoke. Thank God and all the ancient spirits that guard this holy place you are still alive to see it! That is what we call a Dane Dawn."

The Harbledown characters and events are imagined. The twenty day siege of Canterbury by the Danish host ended, so it is recorded, when the raiders got into the city with aid of Aelfmaer, Abbot of St. Augustine's. He was allowed to escape whilst the city and cathedral were burnt. For the people of Canterbury, if the Saxon Chronicles are correct, it was a night of butchery, rape and torture. Archbishop Aelfheah (Alphege) was taken and all but four of his monks murdered. Aelfheah was held for ransom but was eventually beaten to death at the Dane camp at Greenwich. Many of the survivors of the fall of Canterbury were sold as slaves at the Northgate. Harbledown survived but its closeness to Canterbury meant it could not have escaped the attention of the Danes during the siege.

TALE NINE

The Unclean

Randalph felt dizzy. "Not another attack of the fevers please," he fervently prayed, mumbling the words under his cowl. It was hard and painful enough for him to limp down this long hill towards where he had been told the Archbishop Lanfranc had established a refuge for such as he. "Follow the road to Canterburie," he had been told. "It's outside the city but high and fresh, with a holy water well and a skilled monk to tend your pains." This advice had been given by a passing priest who had kindly thrown him a hunk of bread. After soaking it in water and turning it into a pap, Randalph had managed to swallow some down, but the ulcers in his mouth and throat were getting more painful each day and his lips more tender and sore.

"What have I done to deserve such a fate? To become one of the unclean, a leper," he asked himself, over and over. As he tottered along, he scarcely noticed what a bright, sunny, early summer day it was for he kept his head close-covered as the light hurt the skin of his swollen face. Nor did he hear the cheerful birdsong from the thick woods which fringed the ancient road he walked. For him, the days of pain and anguish slid into each other. He was shunned by passers-by, recognised as a leper by his clothing and the staff he leant on. Some threw small coins to him, others scraps of food. He preferred the scraps as no one wanted to take coins *he* had handled.

It was the loneliness, next to the pain, that eroded his spirit. He slept where he could, under hedges, in ruined barns and sheds, in haystacks, but this was dangerous, as he had learned. A group of peasants had discovered him one morning and, in their fear, had driven him off, pelting him with stones and sticks.

As he hauled himself along he thought back over the years. He had first come to this land with William, in the year 1066. He had been one

61

of Odo's men, Bishop Odo of Bayeux, William's half-brother, as much a warrior as a churchman, more so, most said. A brutal, vain and ambitious man, Odo had done well, becoming earl of Kent just six months after we killed Harald and beat the English host. Randalph remembered that battle well, how they had charged uphill again and again at the English shield-wall only to be driven back by hails of spears, throwing axes, even lumps of rock and wood. They were stubborn fighters, these English, but when it came to it they let their courage outrun their good sense. The Norman war host several times had pretended to retreat and always part of the English force spilt downhill in a mad charge and snap, the trap was shut. Randalph, although only eighteen years old and already a seasoned foot-soldier, had been hard pressed to keep up with his lord, especially as the sloping battlefield was wet and slippery with blood. No easy task to charge uphill, wearing a heavy chain-ring shirt, hefting the big shield and carrying a long spear. Still, once in amongst the English, discipline and unthinking resolution had carried the day. Randalph had come to the attention of Odo by taking one of the English warriors full in the belly with his spear, just as he was about to hack down Odo's horse with his fearsome two-handed long axe. Randalph knew his thrust was lucky, but nonetheless was quite happy to receive Odo's thanks for his bravery, especially as he was promoted and given a captured English horse. He recalled too, how he had ridden with William and Odo up this road to Lundun, after Canterburie had surrendered to them. How a group of English leaders had met and knelt to William, how William had eventually entered Lundun in triumph, but only after trekking across country, harrying, pillaging and burning as they went. It took much to cow these English. They still fought on, even years after they had been beaten in battle.

In the twenty years since he had come to this land, as with the others who had sold their swords, Randalph had at first done well for himself. The looting was greatly to his taste, not so much the massacring and torture. But if that was what his liege-lord ordered, then that was what was to be done. Only six years before he had ridden north with Odo to harry the northlands, avenging the massacre of Bishop Walcher and all his men at Raegeheafde (Gateshead). They had laid waste all the land for several days' ride, emptying the countryside, leaving their mark in a way future generations would respect. It was on this campaign he had first begun to notice his health failing. At first he thought it was just old age creeping on. After all, he was thirty-two years old and had travelled far and wide, lived rough on campaigns and collected his share of wounds and bruises in many a battle or skirmish. But the fevers had increased, each becoming more prolonged. Then, to his horror, on his return from the north he noticed the first reddish swellings on his neck and face. These were painful and gradually over the months had spread and hardened. His comrades-in-arms at Odo's strong keep at Hrofesceaster (Rochester), guarding the bridge across the river Miodowaege, had chided him with obscenities and jokes. But for Randolph it was no joke. He had seen this disease before, when he had travelled for a season's fighting in the Roman lands a few years back, and he knew that others who had been south to fight the Moors had returned smitten by this curse. As his condition worsened the hardening red swellings spread to his ears, his nose, his upper arms and thighs. There was no hiding it and he was almost relieved when the keep commander ordered him to leave. By now he was shunned, even by former friends, men he had fought alongside. They turned away, muttering about "God's curse", crossing themselves. For a while he had been allowed to stay in a rickety outhouse close by the keep gate, but even this was too near for comfort for the garrison. So he was ordered away, in shame and disgrace, given a flask of water, a satchel of food and a few coins. No more than that to show for over twenty years of loyal service to his master

He tramped the countryside for weeks, first heading inland, hoping to avoid people and find somewhere he could build a hut and settle and die but he was sent packing everywhere he went. Then he heard of Lanfranc's refuge and set out to find it. And it was, for him, a long march.

Through his dazed mind he realised the road was levelling out and bending. And he remembered. This was where he and the others had hunted through the woods, seeking out and killing Saxon rebels, making an example of them for daring to disrespect the Norman way. That had been good sport, but hot, thirsty work. The memory flitted away as soon as it came. He plodded on. More memories crept back, his time at Canterburie after coming back with Odo's band, all those years ago. He had not thought much of it as a place, full of sullen townspeople and churchmen scuttling about. It was busy enough, with the houses of rich merchants and tradesmen packed closely together in the heart of the town and out along the roads beyond the walls. Many things were made there and the riverside mills were always at work. The cattle market throve. Goods flowed in and out, much from across the seas, brought in up river by the skilful Jewish traders who lived in a close-knit community. The arrival of the Norman overlords did little to change all this. Odo and his chief men were shrewd enough to want to keep the wealth flowing. They did, however, Randalph remembered, impress their power with new stone churches, a strong motte and bailey guarding the road and gate to Dofre (Dover) and, after the Saxon cathedral fortuitously burnt down in A.D. 1067, a grand new Norman-style replacement. They also carved up the local estates and forests for their own use and pleasure. But for all that, Randalph had been bored. This was a rich city but there were no pickings for the likes of him. Life seemed a tedious round of guard duty on the wall in all weathers and long drinking sessions in between. The townsfolk ignored the Norman soldiers as far as possible. He yearned for action and the thrill of plunder. His daydream remembering stopped as he tripped on a stone. He shook his head and looked up.

There, at last, he could see smoke rising above the trees. Squinting through his puffy eyes he could make out a part-built stone church on a hillside, overlooking the road. There were huts grouped round it and figures coming and going, some in monks' habit. He came to a gate, barring a track up the side of the hill. Here stood an elderly monk who beckoned him in, gently taking him by the arm and helping him towards the huts. He was sat down on a bench, questioned and asked to show his disfiguring swellings. "It's God's will, my son," said the old man. "Still, we can care for you, ease your pain, bring you to forgiveness before you die. Whatever you have done, we can gain God's grace for you."

In the coming days Randalph was to find some solace for his pain from the soothing balms and potions the monks made from their extensive hillside herb-garden, using water from the holy well and springs. He was fed and reclothed but was expected to work as well as he could, collecting firewood, cleaning out the pigs, fetching water. They were a mixed lot, this colony of lepers, men and women, young and old, some Saxon, some Norman and former soldiers like himself. They tended to be quiet, reserved, each keeping close their grief, pain and shame at having somewhere, sometime, sinned deeply. The daily routine, the regular prayers, the observances gave a structure to their lives and a sense of purpose.

The monks received some help from a few of the local people, although most kept well away, crossing to pass by on the other side of the road that wound round the refuge. One of these helpers was a woman in her mid-twenties, simple-minded but kind. He learned she was an orphan from the time of the conquest and had stayed childlike ever since.

Randalph thought no more about this until one day, when he was struggling to fill a pitcher with water, she came to his assistance. As she bent to help him her head covering slipped and a crop of white-blond hair was revealed. On the crown of her head, though, was a deep dent, a bald pink patch. She quickly re-covered her head, looking embarrassed.

At that moment Randalph knew his sin, understood why he was being punished. The memory stormed back into his mind. He fell to his knees, sobbing and asking the young woman for forgiveness. She looked at him with amusement. What was this strange man doing, asking her to forgive him. Forgive him for what? Randalph was too choked with emotion and pain to speak so she ran off to fetch the old monk.

Later Randalph was able to explain. He remembered when he had last seen that shock of hair before. It had been as he and some others had ridden out of Canterburie looking for plunder. After the great battle and taking Dofre, William had rested his men up in the city. Inevitably, like their Norsemen forebears, his men had scoured the local countryside, looking for food and loot, cutting down any obstinate Saxons who stood in their way, imposing their will as they chose. It was here, at this very place, Randalph and the others had come. They were wary because of the thick woods that closed in but had spotted a thin plume of smoke rising above the trees. Someone was at home. The armed men soon came across a farmstead and, to their delight, the Saxon family was still there. The man had attempted to hold them off with his spear, whilst his wife stood at his shoulder with a felling-axe. They did not last long. Before torching the house, Randalph had shouldered down the door of an out-shed. Hearing a muffled cry, he reached behind a pile of straw and dragged out a small girl-child, not much more than five years but with white-blond hair. Not giving a second thought, Randalph had clubbed her head with his sword-hilt and thrown her aside. "Too small to be of any use," he had thought. He and his colleagues rode off, happy with their pickings, uncaring about what they had done. Like the rest of the pack he was young and brutal.

Now, in God's good time, Randalph had come to know why he was being punished by his affliction. This simple child-like woman with her angel's hair had survived to help him, to remind him, to bring him to an understanding of the way God worked. Perhaps now he could seek salvation, an end to his misery, wash away his sins and cease to be 'unclean'. Perhaps.

The Norman conquest and other major incidents and places are recorded in history and archaeology. Randalph is an imagined character but his story indicates the well-known on-going brutality of the Norman invasion and the consequent suppression of the Anglo-Saxon peoples, not least in Kent. The scourge of leprosy ended within three centuries but St. Nicholas' church and hospital, now almshouses for the elderly, remains, albeit altered and refurbished.

TALE TEN

Henry's Penance

During the next hundred years the descendants of the Norman conquerors spent much time arguing and fighting amongst themselves, both here and across the Channel, taking time off occasionally to foray into Wales or Scotland. For the mass of the common Saxon folk it was a time to readjust to the new overlords, to come to terms with the loss of their land and the destruction of ancient rights.

Canterbury flourished, with a new castle, a priory, a nunnery and many new churches. Rich merchants and skilled craftsmen, living in solid-built stone houses, bought, sold and made fine jewellery and minted coins as well as manufacturing a wide range of other products. The city spread out well beyond its walls along the main roads. Much of Harbledown was in the Archbishop's Estursete (Westgate) manor, the long strip arable fields farmed by peasants, answerable to their clerical overlords who also kept a strict watch on the use of the forest for unauthorised swine pasturing and illegal hunting. The leper hospital stood on its knoll, overlooking the main London road. Apart from this, little had changed except for the new stone church, St. Michael's. Then, in the late afternoon of Tuesday 29 December A.D. 1170 an event occurred which was to affect Canterbury for centuries to come and, coincidentally Harbledown too. Four of Henry II's knights rode into the city, forced their way into the cathedral and hacked down Archbishop Thomas Becket. Once the King's close friend, he had quarrelled bitterly with his monarch and in a fit of rage Henry cried out to be rid of this turbulent priest. And he was, but at great cost to his royal prestige. Tales of the miracles ascribed to Becket's blood and relics spread rapidly. Four years later Henry II decided it was time to make a gesture of public atonement for his ill-tempered outburst . . .

The old woman hobbled painfully along the lane. Her arthritis was getting worse, not helped by this cool, grey, wet summer. It was early on the twelfth day of July, A.D. 1174, just as dawn was breaking, and the King, Henry II, was coming to the leper hospital church. She had to see him, speak with him, for she had seen two visions in dreams about which he must be told.

"Old Beth", as she was called, lived up in the woods, in a tiny hut, a lonely, solitary existence, kept alive as much by the charity of the local people as by her own skill at seeking out roots, nuts and berries. In other ages she would have been called a witch, but her wisdom and visions had earned her respect and a degree of wary affection. Even the local priest, and those few monks who helped at the leper refuge, grudgingly accepted her and tolerated her ways, but only just.

These were difficult times. Ever since the twenty-one-year-old Henry of Anjou had been crowned king of all the lands from the Scottish border to the Pyrenees twenty years before, there had been war, either in the Welshlands or across the sea in France, even in England itself. It seemed as if the princes, counts and barons were forever rebelling or siding with each other. It had been the same before that, for nineteen long winters, when Simon and Matilda, Henry's mother, had squabbled for the crown. Even Henry's three sons had risen against him the previous year. It was as well the King was a strong, energetic and resilient man, although sometimes his temper got the better of his judgement.

Old Beth knew little of these events of state, only picking up stray bits of news and gossip from passing travellers. These days, since the murder of Archbishop Becket by the King's men, she had noticed an increase in the numbers of folk journeying to Caunterburie, passing along the way across the wooded Biggebery ridge where she lived. This hill was shunned most of the time by the locals, for it was said this was where the ancient ones had lived and it had a reputation for being haunted. This suited Old Beth fine for it meant the villagers only came to see her when it was really important or if they desperately wanted her help.

As she sat at night, looking into her fire, she often had dream visions. She had foretold the death of Becket, describing the rise and fall of the long swords wielded by the four knights, seeing the blades shine and flash in the altar candle-light, then dripping red with steaming blood. At the time she had shared this seeing with the priest at St. Michael's church, months before the event. He had scoffed at her.

"This is exactly why we have built a new church here, on this hilltop, in recent times. To keep such nonsense in its place. That is why we dedicated this church to St. Michael, the slayer of devils. For too long you people here have indulged yourselves in pagan, wicked ways whilst giving lip-service to God. We knew about such practices and the way you folk had quietly corrupted the priests sent here so they turned a blind eye to your strange goings-on. Now you have a real, stone church, built solid in the Norman way. And you have a man of God who will not believe the ramblings of a mad, old woman. Think yourself lucky you are old, otherwise I might be less lenient."

For all that, Old Beth noticed since Becket's death, this priest gave her a wide berth, crossing himself whenever he saw her. Now she had other dreams, but these were for the King himself.

Word had arrived that Henry was coming to do penance, full of remorse at falsely accusing his old friend Thomas a'Becket of treachery and so unleashing the four mad knights who thundered into Caunterburie to rid the King of his quarrelsome archbishop. Mind you, nearly four years after the event was a long time to wait to repent, many thought. Some even reckoned it was because Henry wanted and needed to regain the good feelings and respect of his people. For had not the holy man's blood and relics wrought miracles? Had he not been canonized just a year ago and was now St. Thomas a'Becket? It would be a foolish king who ignored the growing numbers of pilgrims coming to seek God and the sainted martyr's favour. A public show of reconciliation with his old friend, or rather his old friend's remains, should do the trick. Henry was riding overnight, coming all the way from Hamtun.

The old, ragged woman creaked her way to the foot of the steps up to the hospital and sat on a tree stump, pulling her thin cloak over her head. Although the King was not expected until the 8 a.m. Terce service already people were gathering, especially the well-to-do, dressed in their finery. Various monks and other church worthies busied about, making sure the steps and path were clean and dry, no easy task as it was still drizzling with rain and the ground underfoot was mucky. Fresh bundles of twigs and sticks were sent for to spread out to ensure the King walked dry-footed. No one took any notice of Old Beth. She sat quietly humming to herself, but keeping a beady eye open on what was going on.

After a long wait a horse came pounding up, bearing a young squire, announcing, "The King is coming!", and there was a great bustling and jostling as the onlookers sorted out who would stand where, in order of rank and dignity. There were a few harsh words and grumbles but soon all was ready. By now the rain had ceased and a warming sun broke through the clouds. Old Beth eased her aching bones and stood up, leaning on her staff. A pompous-looking prelate noticed her and had just motioned one of his minions to move her on when a distant trumpet call pealed out and the clatter of cantering horses was heard.

Round the bend in the road came a splendid sight – brightly dressed outriders, armoured knights and soldiers, with pennants, lances, shields, a shining, jangling, jingling but mud-spattered column of fifty or more horsemen and at their head, riding unhelmeted, the King himself. He halted at the foot of the steps and sat looking around, acknowledging the cheering crowd. A square but agile man even though he was now forty-one years old and showing grey hair, he slid lithely from his saddle and stood, waiting for his official welcome from the hospital chaplain.

He was led up the steps to the chaplain's abode to refresh himself, then to pray in the St. Nicholas' church. It was here the public penance would begin. Meantime, the lepers, the men dressed in russet gowns with hoods, the women in loose gowns with black veils, had been rounded up and sent to the other end of the hospital grounds, there to await the King. They now numbered nearly a hundred, their ranks swollen by returning afflicted Crusaders. Henry would come near to them, but not too close, and scatter alms for them as a King should. Such was the fear and superstition about leprosy that the welcoming crowd made no attempt to follow the King and his party into the hospital grounds. All except Old Beth. She knew enough about this cursed disease from observation alone to realise that you couldn't catch anything other than fleas from these wretches except by very close intimate physical contact.

She hobbled up the steps, a familiar and harmless figure to the hospital monks, and went to stand near the church door. The flint-stone church was surrounded by armed soldiers, their swords point down, forming a protective iron-ring for their King. Even on God's land in these times he took no chances.

Henry was not long cleaning up and shortly emerged, now rid of his armour and dressed in sombre clothing. As the slow procession climbed the shallow steps to the church Beth fell to her knees and in a surprisingly powerful voice for one so frail-looking called out, "My King, my King. I must speak with you!"

There was a horrified intake of breath from the assembled clerics and royal attendants. This was too much. A burly sergeant-at-arms leapt forward, his arm raised to knock the old woman out of the way.

"Hold fast!" snapped Henry. "Remember today I do penance, today she is as worthy as me in the eyes of God."

This took some of the onlookers aback. Still if the King wanted to act in this humble and uncharacteristic way, who were they to disagree?

"Speak, old woman. But make it brief."

"My Lord King, what I have to say is for your ears only."

"Mm, well then, step inside the church door and I will listen. But be brief."

Making certain she was carrying no hidden knife or other weapon, the monks shepherded Beth into the dimly-lit church and withdrew, leaving her alone with Henry. She had never been in this church before and was amazed by the brilliant red, greens, blues and golds of the wall-paintings which covered every surface. This was indeed a beautiful place.

"Speak," commanded Henry.

Beth recounted her visions of the great church burning, of flames reaching high into the sky but the remains of the holy Becket would survive. She had seen them rise up through the flames. This would be soon. But the worse was that the Holy City, Jerusalem, would fall to the heathen, and before Henry's own death. This would be not many years from now and would cause great distress throughout Christendom. "Be ready, my Lord King, for such events could shake the throne."

Henry stood silent, mulling over her words.

"Thank you, old one, but speak to no man or woman of what has passed between us. Now leave me to pray for it seems I have much to pray about."

Beth left Henry and hobbled off but decided, as it was now such a fine day and as she had shared her far-seeing with the king, to walk on down to the St. Dunstan's church. With luck she might get a ride back on a wagon.

She sat for several hours outside St. Dunstan's church, waiting. During this time she was well supplied with gifts of food and small coins from passers-by, so much so that her leather bag was overflowing. Suddenly the crowd lining each side of the London road set up a cry: "The King comes!" Then they fell silent, for there, walking down the middle of the road, flanked by monks and soldiers, came Henry.

He looked stern-faced, not downcast, but suitably reverent, folk thought. He entered St. Dunstan's, noticing Old Beth near the doorway. He gave her a half-smile and a nod of recognition. After more prayers and chanting he emerged, now wearing a rough woollen shirt, covered with a pilgrim's cloak. He was barefooted, as was right for a penitent. Naturally the City fathers, having been told in advance of the King's intention, had made sure the roadway was swept as clean as possible of dung and other refuse, but even so it was a popular gesture, the sort of thing people remembered. To see the King walking barefooted and in a simple shirt: now that was something!

As Beth heard of it later, Henry had walked all the way to the Cathedral, being symbolically scourged the last part of the way by a hundred or so priests and bishops. The penance was done. Old Beth had also done what her inner voice had commanded. As for Henry, he left Canterbury with much on his mind.

Old Beth is obviously an imagined character whilst Henry II's visit is recorded.

Two months after his penance, in September, A.D. 1174, the Cathedral choir was gutted by fire but Becket's body, resting in the crypt, was spared. Henry ruled for another fifteen difficult years, long enough to see Jerusalem fall to Saladin and his Muslim armies in A.D. 1187. Yet another Crusade was called for. It is thought St. Michael's Norman church was built around A.D. 1150. Before he left St. Nicholas' hospital Henry made a gift of twenty silver marks to be paid every year out of the royal dues from Canterbury. It is still paid, now by the City Council.

TALE ELEVEN

Bobbe-up-and-doun

In the years following Becket's martyrdom Canterbury became the focus of religious activity on a Europe-wide scale with the church authorities seizing the opportunity to encourage pilgrims to flood in from afar, bringing with them great prosperity for the city and the church. The age of the Canterbury Pilgrims had begun and Harbledown stood astride two major pilgrim ways, from London and along what is now called the North Downs Way. But in many other ways this was a time of stress, with continual warfare in France as the English kings strove to take, hold and reclaim territory. Then came the Black Death, wiping out at least a third or more of the population, disrupting life in town and village alike. It took years to recover, especially in the countryside where fields were abandoned and the forests began to creep back in. Harbledown could not have escaped the plague's scourge but maintained its identity, not least because of its position on the main road from Dover to London. The great and powerful continued to pass through . . .

The cavalcade of armoured knights and their attendant squires, bodyguards and pack-horses almost filled the width of the rutted road, splashing mud onto bystanders and travellers alike as they thundered past. Over a hundred in number, the horsemen were an impressive sight, not least the King's son Edward, the Black Prince, magnificent in his fine armour, highly polished and gleaming in the late autumn sun. Alongside him rode another fine figure, but smaller and looking miserable. This must be John, King of France, captured at the battle of Poitiers a few weeks before, now being take to the Tower of London to meet with the English King, Edward III.

Once again the Black Prince had outsmarted the French, striking deep inland from the English-held port of Bordeaux, bringing them to battle

73

finally at Poitiers. Here a skilful combination of long-bow archers and dismounted men-at-arms had broken the charge of the French knights, throwing them into confusion and disarray. "Like Crècy all over again," Joan's Uncle Will had told her. And he should know, for he had fought in that battle ten years before, losing the use of his left arm to a French sergeant's sword-slash.

"My, that Prince Edward is a handsome man," thought Joan, standing on tiptoe to get a better sight of him. "Lucky the maids who find his favour." Joan was scarce fifteen years old but already well-filled out and aware of her prettiness. She lived here at Herbeldoun, up towards where the common land began. Now there was just her and her father Edgar, a freeman, a silent but kindly man, grey and lined even though he had not yet reached the age of forty. A skilled craftsman, he worked the local smithy, getting his charcoal from the nearby forest.

Until seven years ago they had been a full family, husband, wife, two sons and two daughters. Then came the dreaded plague, the Black Death. Joan still woke in the middle of the night, fearfully remembering those dreadful days when Death stalked the land and came to their cottage. It was as if God had turned his back on them. First there was the poor harvest, with the rain and low cloud day after day, all through the summer up until Christ Mass. As if to compound the hardship already endured, word came of a great sickness sweeping the land, moving north and east from the sea-ports down in the southwest. People were dying by their thousands, no one, high or low born, was spared once the disease took hold. Avoiding contact with those afflicted seemed the only way to survive, but was no guarantee.

It was early in spring, a cold, snowy time with the fields still frost-frozen and iron-hard when they heard that the pestilence had arrived in Caunterburie. It was spreading like wildfire amongst the close-packed houses and pilgrim inns, respecting neither monastery nor abbey, rich or poor, pilgrim or townsfolk. Whole families were being wiped out, the grave-diggers couldn't keep pace with the cartloads of corpses coming out of the city. Even so, Edgar and his eldest son, twelve-year-old John, had to go down to the town to collect a pack-horse load of iron for the smithy. As the merchant lived outside the walls, Edgar reckoned it should be safe enough for them.

They returned white-faced and anxious. "It is like hell down there," said Edgar grimly. "They were boarding up houses, whether the folk in them be dying or dead. I was told the market-place is empty, there are dead in the streets and rats everywhere. We didn't venture past the gates to see. God save us all. We must stay close to home and pray."

But unknowingly John had brought the plague home with him, passed on by the merchant's son he had been sporting with whilst their fathers agreed a fair price. The boy had coughed and spluttered all through their play. Two days after returning home, John complained of a sore throat. His nose was running and soon his head ached badly. He quickly developed a raging fever and, to his parents despair, ugly, dark, bruise-like blotches appeared on his skin, followed speedily by the dreaded swelling lumps in his groin and under his armpits. He died in pain within three days, but by then the two other children were running a fever, although miraculously not Joan, perhaps because as the smallest and youngest she was kept right away from John and not asked to help tend him. Her mother also succumbed and within ten days just Edgar and Joan were left. Other local families fared better, others worse. By the time the pestilence had passed on, heading remorselessly for London, the midlands and the north at least a third of the local people had died. That spring fields were left untended, weeds grew everywhere, livestock broke loose and wandered the woods. Trade fell off sharply and there were few travellers.

Caunterburie, the populous, thriving, bustling city of just six months before was now a ghostly place. Many shops, houses and workplaces were empty, boarded-up; there were few people in the refuse-choked streets, trade was slack, the pilgrims no longer came in any number and the inns were empty. But somehow life returned to something like normal and by the time summer came Edgar had part recovered from his grief and knew for sure the Black Death had departed, for the pilgrims had begun to trickle back, many to give thanks at Becket's shrine for being spared. Two years later when Joan was ten and old enough to be allowed to go down to the village on her own to watch the travellers pass by, the old road was again thick with pilgrims, young and old, rich and poor, some travelling singly, some sick and crippled, others in noisy, chattering groups, all heading to or returning from seeking the holy martyr's blessing. Gradually many of the neglected fields were brought back into cultivation, though some stayed untended for years and the forest began to reclaim them, edging in, season by season.

For Joan, life was not always easy but neither was it particularly hard. Her father made a good living, including from moulding hundreds of pilgrim badges and trinkets which found an eager market in the city.

Since the death of his wife and other children he seemed to seek solace in work, indulging Joan with fine clothing and baubles, but insisting she kept the house, made meals and tended the chickens and two pigs they kept. He cared for the two horses and their milch-cow. Neither father nor daughter was much of a hand at the vegetable garden and this became a weed-patch.

Joan felt lonely. There were few left locally of her own age, a shortage of likely lads to eye up and down as a future husband: none, according to her father, reached the mark he expected for his daughter. He did warn her, however, to beware the pilgrims. "They may be on a holy quest but for some they seem to want to sin deeply on their journey so they can be even more penitent when they kneel to pray for forgiveness. Rogues and vagabonds, that's what I call them. You watch out, my girl. Sweet, honeyed words and betrayal often go together, especially from young gentlemen who are just passing through. Here today and gone tomorrow, with you left holding the baby." Still, that didn't stop her looking and dreaming of what might be, or even might never be.

"There are some fine young men riding past now," she thought. Some were tall and willowy, their wealth and rank shown by their fine bright clothing, feathered hats and shining belts and buckles. Others were, she judged, more manly but not so beautiful; armoured men, hardened by campaigning, but bearing themselves with a muscular confidence and the swagger of fighting men who had won. As they rode by she noticed one young gentleman, perhaps about sixteen years of age, fresh-faced, finely dressed but not as gaudily as some of the others. He caught her eye, smiled and gave a slight bow in her direction. She felt her heart flutter at the flattery. Then, to her joy, she saw the head of the mounted column was pulling into the paddock close by the lane leading up to the ancient well. What was happening, why were they stopping?

The answer soon became clear. The Prince had decided to rinse his head in the holy water. If truth be told he was feeling hot and dirty. His scalp itched and wearing heavy armour during months of summer campaigning had left several nasty, raw patches which were exceedingly sore. Also he stank of sweat. What he needed was a good wash down with cold, clear water and if it were blessed holy water, so much the better. Normally he would have stopped off in Caunterburie on his journey from Doufre to Lundun but that would have meant much ceremony, droning speeches of welcome from the city worthies, prolonged prayers with the archbishop, and some lengthy feasting. He wanted to get his captive John to the Tower and safely under lock and key as speedily as possible. So he had sent word ahead to the city to say he would come in by the Riding Gate and pass through without stopping to the West Gate. The city elders were to keep the streets clear and apart from a brief formal welcome when he entered he would have no time to halt. These were great matters of state which demanded all haste. To impress the citizens he had ordered his men to ride in full armour and put on a fine show of royal English strength. They could shed some of the weightier items once they were clear of the city.

As Joan watched, the riders dismounted, some of the heavily-armoured knights having to be helped out of their saddles with much heaving and grunting. The horses were led off to the nearby stream for a drink whilst a dozen or so men-at-arms formed a loose circle around the Prince, himself surrounded by pages and attendants helping him strip off his armour. Knights stood around talking and bantering whilst their pages unbuckled leg and arm plates. Others went off to relieve themselves in a nearby ditch, a complicated exercise for anyone wearing full armour. Joan modestly averted her eyes from this activity, allowing her sense of propriety to overcome her natural curiosity. She did, however, notice the young man who had caught her fancy coming towards her, or so she hoped. She pretended not to look at him, but he came over to her and doffed his cap. She made a small curtsey, as was proper, and stood demurely, her eyes down. After a short pause, which for Joan seemed endless, he spoke. It was, she thought, a Lundun voice but courteous and gracious for all that. He asked her who she was, did she live hereabouts, what was her name?

Joan looked up, finding herself blushing, and stuttered out an answer. The young man laughed, not unkindly, and told her not to be afraid. He apologised for being so forward and inquisitive, but that was his nature. He then went on to explain he had been a page at the King's court and had been sent with others to welcome the Prince and his royal captive at Doufre and help escort them to Lundun. Now the Prince had decided to stop and wash at the holy well. Was this the place where the lepers had lived, were there any left, had the plague wiped them out, who lived in those huts around the church? He stopped and laughed. "There, I'm doing it again. Always questions, questions. One day I shall write a great book telling of all I know."

Joan found herself laughing with him and soon the barrier of rank disappeared. They began chatting like any two young people, about this and that, about the latest fashion in hats, which sorts of sweetmeats they liked, how funny the fat priest looked as he waddled along. Before they knew it a trumpet pealed out. The Prince was making ready to leave.

"I must go," said the young man. "Thank you for talking to me, Joan. I shall not forget you." He squeezed her hand, made a courtly bow and turned to go, but paused.

"One more question, one last question." He laughed as he said it. "What do you call this place?"

"Why, it is Herbeldoun, sir, but we call it 'Bobbe-up-and-doun' because of all these little hills hereabouts."

"Thank you again sweet Joan. I shall remember that name well," replied the young Geoffrey Chaucer as he went off to join the Prince.

The effect of the Black Death on Canterbury and the surrounding countryside is well documented. Joan and her family are imagined but the story of the Black Prince washing at the well in A.D. 1356, whilst not verified, has come down through the ages. There is also a tale that when he was dying, Prince Edward sent for water from the holy well or spring. He is buried in Canterbury Cathedral. Geoffrey Chaucer was with the Prince when he brought John of France to London and in his great book, the famous Canterbury Tales, *refers to Harbledown as 'Bobbe-up-and-doun' in the section 'Words of Divers of the Pilgrims', preceding the Manciple's Tale.*

TALE TWELVE

The Long March

A generation after the Black Death its effects were still visible in the countryside, with once abandoned fields needing to be reclaimed from the forest, deserted cottages crumbling and a shortage of labour. The wars in France continued, becoming more and more of a financial drain with little to show in return. Canterbury's strategic importance and closeness to the enemy across the Channel meant its walls had to be repaired and Archbishop Sudbury set about financing the building of the great Westgate which still stands today. He had also set in motion the building of the huge new nave in the Cathedral. But it was not Sudbury's private fortune which was to foot the bill, rather the tithes and rents which came from the church-owned properties and land in and around the city. Sudbury was understandably not popular with many local town or country folk, even more so as he was the King's Chancellor and author of the detested Poll Tax, introduced to raise money to pay for the unsuccessful wars in France. Resentment grew and festered and in A.D. 1381 spilt over into action . . .

Will straightened his back, groaned and wiped his brow with the back of his hand. The summer heat beat on his stocky shoulders, sweat ran down inside his coarse shirt. It was Saturday, the eighth day of June, 1381, and here he was, working alongside his father, Abel, grubbing out an obstinate oak stump, a labour required of them to enable the great field to be extended. Here at Herbaldoune the church held most of the land and now a generation after the Black Death had swept through the countryside the priests wanted the abandoned fields brought into cultivation, the creeping Bleane forest pushed back to its old edge.

Will felt resentful. He wanted to be down in the town with his uncle, Robert Toneford. The city was abuzz with rumour and seething with excitement. Last night news had come that a large host of men led by Watte Teghelere had taken Maidestoune and freed the holy man, John Ball, and were coming on to Caunterburie. Great events were happening and here he was like a yoked ox, grunting and heaving to shift this cursed stump. And all for the greater riches of the already rich. As Uncle Rob had explained to them, this Archbishop Simon of Sudbury, now the King's Chancellor, was a grasping vainglorious man, riding on the backs of the poor. Not only was he building his massive new nave at the Church of St. Thomas with money squeezed out of poor folk, but his Poll Tax was the final insult. "And to pay for the King's adventures in France, whilst folk like us groan under the burden and saw nothing of benefit."

"I've had enough of this," Will said to his father. "I'm off to the town to see Uncle Rob."

His father nodded. "Be careful son, these are dangerous times." They were indeed for only three days before the King's men, led by John Legge, had been sent packing by a huge crowd of townsfolk, for daring to come to impose Sudbury's writ on the city. Will had watched the frightened men pound their horses up the hill on the road through the hamlet and past the family cottage as they escaped. He had joined in the jeering and stone-throwing as they passed, their faces white with fear and dust, their horses panting and gasping. The hamlet of Herbaldoune nestled under the brow of the hill, close by the church but across the road from where the leper houses had stood.

"Don't be afraid father. I'm old enough to fend for myself." At seventeen Will was fully grown, well-muscled from hard labouring and well-skilled with the quarter staff, the bow, the long knife and, if need be, his felling-axe. Although forbidden to bear arms as mere bondsmen, nevertheless the old skills of weapon handling had been passed secretly down the generations since the Normans came and stole the land.

Will walked rapidly downhill, past the Archbishop's gallows with its crow-pecked, dangling corpse, standing where the road bore off to the left, then on across the fields, shortcutting to the newly completed Westgate. This was another of Sudbury's costly schemes which had caused resentment amongst local folk. Today there was no watch on guard to check the jostling throng. Rumour ran rife. The countryside was in an uproar. Great houses had been taken and their wealth distributed amongst the poor. Over in Essex the people had risen. All across the county prisons were emptied of those who had been falsely locked away. Rochester castle had been taken. The King would have to listen to the rightful voice of his subjects, young as he was, rather than the serpent words of the mighty who ruled in his name, especially Sudbury.

"Wait 'til Watte Teghelere and Jack Straw gets here, then we'll see. They're coming, they're coming!" was on everyone's lips.

Will headed up the main street to the tavern where he knew he would find his uncle. The streets were ablock with people standing in groups, talking and arguing fiercely. There were tradesmen of all kinds, with some from outlying villages, farmworker bondsmen like himself, even some poor priests. He ducked through the low, dark doorway and spotted Uncle Rob in his favourite corner, holding forth to a gang of cronies including John Herbaldoune of Winchepe. Will grabbed a mug of ale and slid on to the bench next to his uncle.

The talk was long and loud, about injustices old, new, real and imagined. It soon became clear to Will that something was being hatched – a way of settling scores with some of the city's rich and powerful men, Bailiffs like Thomas Holte, John Tebbe and especially John Tece. The angry group finally decided to wait until the people's host arrived.

The next day, Trinity Sunday, Will stayed close to home. The local priest, William Savage, rushed through the morning's service, his fat jowls quivering with anxiety. Duty done, Will and his younger brother Tom took to the woods, up in the Bleane, hunting; well, poaching, if truth be told. That night Will slept restlessly.

The sun rose behind the hill to a bright, clear day. Will was up with the dawn chorus but there was to be no work today. He had already agreed with his uncle to go to wait for the great host by the old trackway which came over the hills from the southwest. It was mid-morning however before they heard the far-off singing as the long column emerged from the woods. There must have been four thousand men, and some women, a mighty throng, old and young, skilled men and peasants, some on horseback, some armed with sword or spear, others with staves, axes, bows, sickles, billhooks or even longknives or scythes lashed to stout poles. They marched purposively and cheerfully, pausing only on the crest of the hill where they could look down on the city below them. A loud cheer went up – and on they went, led by a tall, broad man, Watte Teghelere, and a small, black-robed priest, the holy John Ball, mounted on an ass. These were a different kind of pilgrim.

Will and his uncle fell in at the rear of the column. Soon they were entering the Westgate, where crowds of excited, jubilant townspeople greeted them. It was like a fair-day, thought Will, with people singing, drinking and dancing in the streets. But there was serious business to attend to, his uncle reminded him. Without pausing, the host went straight on to the Church of St. Thomas, their faces now grim and unsmiling. They filed quietly into the great church just as the noon High Mass began. Bareheaded, their weapons grounded, the whole body of men and women knelt and then with one great voice called on the assembled monks to elect one of their own number to be archbishop, to replace he who is traitor. They then left and went into the city, filling the streets and crying out for the mayor and bailiffs, who quickly came running. Each was made to swear in good will to be faithful and loyal to King Richard and the Commons of England. "For our complaint is not with the King, but with those who ill-treat us falsely in his name," said Tegehelere. It was then that another man, a John Hales of Malling, leapt up onto the cart alongside Tegehelere and cried out for the names of traitors. The mood of the crowd changed.

Now men and women alike shouted the names of those they hated – or feared: "Tebbe", "de Medmenham", "Holte", "Oteryngton", "de Hoo", "Garwenton", "Fog" and "Tece". Another cry went up: "To the Archbishop's palace!" The crowd surged and seethed, then determined knots broke away, heading for the homes of traitors, to the palace, to the town hall and the castle keep. The looting and revenge began in earnest.

Will found himself swept along through the narrow streets with his uncle, heading for John Tebbe's house and it was here he witnessed the full wrath of men he knew otherwise to be peaceful and God-fearing. Breaking down the door, John London of Otenhill, together with Henry Whyte and Will Cymekin, both Canterbury men, rushed in and emerged with the kicking, struggling Tebbe. Whyte and Cymekin held him down and with one blow of his axe, London beheaded him. The house was then ransacked, stripped from top to bottom.

Word spread that others had been executed, that Holte's house in Westgate had been sacked, as had Sir Tom Fog's manor, whilst at de Medmenham's place the rolls of names used for collecting the Poll Tax had been burned.

"We must find Tece," said Uncle Rob, but his house was shuttered and empty. "The rat has run, but I will have him!" growled Rob.

Will knew well the feud between the two men ran deep and was longstanding, ever since Tece wrongly accused his uncle of defaulting on a payment for some iron nails. As a result Rob had had an ear cropped, marking him forever as a cheat.

The rest of that momentous Monday passed quickly. Will found himself dashing back and forth, caught up in the excitement and confusion of a city in revolt. By evening things quieted down so he and his uncle decided to trek back across the fields to Herbaldoune, exhausted but elated. They knew that the next day the host would begin the long march to London to see the King, aiming to camp on the Bleakenheathe before descending on London City. Will wanted to go but his uncle, and later his father, cautioned against it.

"We still have our local rats to flush out," said Rob. "Stay here and help me find Tece. Tomorrow will be enough." Will shook his head obstinately, his father shrugged his shoulders, his mother bit her lip. Will had decided.

Next morning he stood waiting by the roadside at the top of the hill by the church. He had a pouch of food, a skin bag of water – and his felling-axe. He was ready to see the King, to kneel and swear allegiance but first Sudbury and all the other traitors would be thrown down.

The column swung up the hill, cheerful, excited but determined. A formidable force of men, and a few women, from all kinds of backgrounds and with all kinds of skills, they were united in one purpose, to throw off the yoke of oppression of the many by the few. Will made his farewells and joined the throng.

"Find Tece and settle with him!" he called back over his shoulder.

"I will, I will!" came the reply.

Of the characters in this tale only Will and his family are fiction, the rest feature in contemporary records, as do the incidents. Will would have marched the sixty miles to London, arriving with the rest of the people's army on Blackheath late in the evening of Wednesday 12 June. The rebels from both Kent and Essex took London on the Thursday, sacked, looted and burned the palaces and houses of those they saw as enemies of the realm, and beheaded Sudbury and others on Friday 14 June. The next day Richard II met Wat Tyler (Tegehelere) and others at Smithfield. Tyler was trapped and treacherously cut down. Hungry and dispirited the rebels dispersed. Within a few days the King ordered the suppression of the rebellion. Many were hunted down and executed. Will likely never returned home, falling to the King's men at the final battle of Billericay.

Meanwhile in Canterbury on Tuesday 11 June, John Tece was caught, dragged from his horse and killed. Those accused of killing him were John Cook of Canterbury, Henry Alleyn of Chartham, John Grenelef of Petham, John Bromfeld of Elham, and Robert Toneford of Harbledown. All were executed. As late as 1 July the people of Canterbury were still resisting the royal commissioners of peace. The embers of freedom dimmed, but did not go out.

TALE THIRTEEN

The Coming of Cade

Two generations on and England was still embroiled in wars across the Channel, but for Canterbury these were changing times. The revival after the Black Death and the Peasants' Revolt saw pilgrims flocking in, bringing wealth and prosperity to some, but not to all. For the poorer families, crowded together in the disease-ridden riverside parishes, life was often unhealthy, miserable and short. For the wealthiest families, however, it was a time to build fine timber-frame houses whilst new inns, taverns and lodging houses sprang up to cater for the pilgrims. The poor, needy, sick and homeless, pilgrim and local alike, were helped by the various church establishments, probably providing five hundred years ago more assistance to the homeless poor than is available today. Harbledown shared in the boom period, providing for the passing trade and from the demands from the city. Outwardly little had changed although increasingly fields were smaller, with more farms scattered around. There was a gradual shift away from reliance on grain growing. But in A.D. 1420 came a downturn with declining trade, particularly affecting small businesses like pottery, leather, textiles and clothing. The effects would have been felt in nearby Harbledown with falling demand for local produce and fewer travellers. Discontent began to rumble again but this time Canterbury was well in the control of the local worthies, some of whose grandfathers had suffered a nasty shock in 1381 . . .

John ducked behind a tree and held his breath. Should he dare go any nearer, he wondered. He knew he was doing wrong coming here to see, but his ten-year-old's curiosity had got the better of him. He had slipped out of the family cottage, just down the hill from the church of St. Michael, here at Herbeldoun, soon after rising. He ought to have been heading in the opposite direction, up into the common land woods, to

85

collect kindling but the noise of stamping and neighing horses, the clink of arms and armour, the murmur of voices and occasional shouts together with the smell from dozens of fires had drawn him the other way.

It was the year A.D. 1450, June, just after Trinity. "A hot summer with hot work afoot," his father had said. John's father, a stocky, slow but powerful man had only recently returned from the wars in France – "the defeats in France," he called them. Unlike many who had crossed the Channel with King Henry VI to avenge French insolence, reclaim lost lands and gain rich pickings, he had a home to return to. Many others, less fortunate and empty-handed, some maimed, now tramped the countryside, begging or thieving. They were much dissatisfied with the King and their lot – unpaid and, as it seemed to them, unwanted and reviled across the land. They had been badly led and ill-used. Normandy had been lost to the French. Disquiet with the Lancastrian King's rule ran deep throughout the nation not least down in Caunterburie itself. Already, back in January, there had been a minor rebellion, when a group of men had attacked the St. Radigund's hospice, near the Northgate. But the City fathers had learned a sharp lesson from the great rising just two generations before. They had acted quickly and firmly, arresting the mob's leader, one Cheyne, known locally as "Blewbeard". There were those who said the city dignitaries sided with the King because he had given them a City Charter a few years before, strengthening their powers and privileges. "Buying them in," John's father said. "Some men would sell their soul to become Mayor or Sheriff." These worthy men had scuttled quickly to declare their allegiance to King Henry but now they faced an even bigger challenge.

A few weeks before Jack Cade, who claimed noble connections and that he had fought under the Duke of York, had led a rising of men of status, mainly from West Kent and the Weald. They were insisting the King did something about a number of discontents and wrongs, embodied in the Kentish Complaint. Misrule of the country and county, injustices inflicted by the corrupt application of the law, the oppressive and extortionate behaviour of Lord Say, Constable of Dover Castle, the bribery and intimidation surrounding the elections of Knights of the Shire – all featured in their list of grievances. Underlying everything, however, was a general distrust of the King's rule and the resentment at the general state of affairs, especially poor trade.

So it was on this bright, breezy June day, young John crouched behind a tree, peeping cautiously at the scene before him. All across the great meadow which sloped downhill from the edge of St. Michael's churchyard towards St. Dunstan's, was a mass of tents, wagons, horse-lines, campfires, men and boys, some grouped around quietly talking and joking, cleaning and sharpening weapons, others practicing sword-play, others tending horses. Colourful pennants snapped in the wind, smoke rose and sped away, the sun glinted off brightly polished armour and shields.

John had never seen so many men gathered together – his father had told him they numbered some four thousand. And these were not poor folk, although he could see many who were dressed in the dull browns and greens of commoners. Some were attired in fine, brightly coloured clothes, others wore shining armour breast-plates. There were squires, many respected gentlemen and even three Sheriffs in this host it was said.

They had all arrived the day before, men on horses and on foot, with wagons and pack-horses, clattering and creaking up and over the hill on the road to the meadow where they set up camp. John's father had told his family, especially his daughters, to keep close to the cottage and speak to no man. He knew well, from his own soldiering, the ways of fighting men when on the march. He had stood firm and solid at the cottage door, a stout staff in his hand, watching the column pass and had, with due courtesy, willingly sold some old hens to one of the passing squires. He had also brought in all their livestock close to the cottage as dusk fell and stood guard throughout the night. "Hungry bellies make for thieving hands," he told his family. That night the roadside inn, the Duke's Head, did a roaring trade, with groups of drunken men rolling up the hill long after dark, shouting and singing on their way back to camp.

As John watched, a trumpet call rang out from the centre of the encampment. Suddenly the camp sprang to life, everyone assembling around a cart on which stood a bare-headed man wearing a breast-plate and holding a sword. He raised his sword and there was silence. Even from here, up on the edge of the meadow, John could hear his powerful voice. The man, Jack Cade it must be, thought John, started by reminding them why they were here, of their grievances and of wrongs to be righted. He told them to assemble, fully armed and in good order, for now they were to march down to the city, to the Westgate, to demand entrance and the allegiance of the City Fathers and citizens. It took some time for the column to sort itself out, but then, with Cade and other finely dressed men, all horsed, at its head, the strong force moved slowly onto the road, turning at St Dunstan's church to the way to the city gates.

John could no longer contain his curiosity. He sped down, across the meadow, through the camp, dodging and weaving past tents, fires and wagons, skipping over piles of horse dung until, breathless, he caught up with the tail of the march. By now, Cade and the other leaders had reached the city to find the bridge up and the great wooden gates shut firm. The towers were lined with armed, grim-faced men, with Mayor Clifton and the City dignitaries standing high (and well protected) on the battlements immediately above the gates. The column halted and fanned out along the river banks, facing the walls.

John, being small and nimble, slipped his way between the ranks of men and horses, close towards where Cade sat, gazing up at the gate towers. John noticed all the houses and cottages lining the road were barred and shuttered for there was no warm welcome here, unlike when the great rising had happened. Squeezing himself into a doorway, John strained his ears to hear what was happening. Some of the men around him started to shout up to those on the walls to "Lower the bridge!", "Open the gates!", "Join us in our crusade!", whilst others just waved their swords.

Cade turned in his saddle and raised his right arm for silence. Dismounting, he stood immediately facing the closed gates and in a loud voice formally called for the surrender of the city. Mayor Clifton hesitated and replied that he and the City Fathers needed time to consider, to which request Cade graciously agreed. The be-robed and be-chained group withdrew out of sight and the waiting began. The sun rose high in the sky, the wind dropped and the day dragged on, long, hot and tiring. Some of the horses became restless and were led away, men began to sit and doze or wander off for a drink from the river or to relieve themselves. Even John, for all his young years, realised this was the wrong way to go about things. The air became thick with smells, of sweating men and horses, stale clothing, sour leather, horse-droppings and urine.

After what had been three hours, well towards noon, there was a stir on the battlements, Mayor Clifton and his retinue had returned. Their answer was a clear "No". They had played the game craftily, reckoning a long wait in the hot sun would take away any fighting edge this host might have. By now Cade and his followers had come to the same conclusion. Caunterburie was not for them, this time. But Cade needed to rally his men so called to them they would waste no more time here. "Let these faint-hearts stew in their city, we shall return to camp, make ready and march on London, to Blackenheath." Which they did with much grumbling and bad grace. On the way a drunken group of them pillaged houses and murdered several owners who were foolish enough to stand against them – and this at Boughton-under-Blene, just a few miles up the road. Herbeldoun had survived again.

John crept home that afternoon, not forgetting to bring an armful of kindling which he had gathered up coming back through the bustling camp. To his surprise his father was not angry at his admission of disobedience but whilst keeping a stern face seemed to be rather pleased with his son's story. "At least you seem to have learned something, so all was not wasted. This Cade, by what you tell me, is no real leader. He let the moment pass and will fail again. He is no better a leader than those we had in France – long on words and short on sense."

John remembered these words well when news came some weeks later that the rebellion had collapsed. Cade was dead, his followers dispersed and hunted down. Early the next year, after the trials, Caunterburie had its own harvest of heads, mass hangings which John went to see. Those hung were mostly common folk for the men with wealth and status had gained the King's pardon. "'twas ever thus," said John's father ruefully, recalling what had happened to his great-uncle Rob after the last rising.

The Cade rebellion is well documented historically, as is the location of the rebel camp downhill from Harbledown village and the Mayor's refusal to surrender the city. The Duke's Head tavern, recorded in A.D. 1416, stood on the site of Pear Tree Cottage. John is an imagined character.

The long and bloody "War of the Roses" between the Lancastrians and the Yorkists got underway in earnest just five years later. Several times in the years following Cade's rising both King Henry VI and King Edward IV and their queens visited Canterbury. Rather than stay in the tight-packed, unhealthy city, they chose to camp high up on the edge of the Blean forest, close to Harbledown in large temporary buildings erected around a huge tent called "le Hale". Perhaps the present-day Duke's Meadow which rises up near Hall Place is where the royal encampment was located.

TALE FOURTEEN

To Bow the Knee

A century passed, bringing change, new styles of housing, different farming methods and crops, and a final loosening of the medieval bondage for the countryfolk. Down in Canterbury Henry VIII's quarrel with the Pope brought about the dissolution of the monasteries and the Reformation. Friaries and nunneries were dissolved and sold off, Becket's shrine obliterated, St. Augustine's abbey unroofed and dismantled. Pilgrims no longer came but Canterbury survived with its contracted population topped up by families moving in from the surrounding countryside. The city held on as it was still the focal market town for East Kent, providing a range of services, including education. It was here Christopher Marlow, born in A.D. 1564, went to school. Many fine townhouses were built and since A.D. 1497 the city and surrounding countryside had been dominated by the cathedral's majestic Bell Harry tower. Canterbury also benefited from developing trade and commerce across the Channel and with the Low Countries. The city was now run by stern, anti-clerical Protestants. To be a Catholic was to be thought traitorous.

Harbledown had also changed. Beamed houses and cottages appeared and fine country houses like Hall Place and the Polres Court manor house were built. A windmill dominated the skyline at the top of Mill Lane. Small orchards of apples and cherries gave a new checkered pattern to the countryside and hop-gardens were beginning to appear. Up towards Rough Common the edge of the Blean forest had been pushed back. New inns were built along the London Road. St. Nicholas' hospital had long become almshouses for the respectable sick and needy. Some of its lands were let to independent farmers. But Reformation begat counter-Reformation and when Henry's Catholic daughter Mary came to the throne in A.D. 1553 to be Protestant was to be treasonable . . .

91

Giles wiped his nose on the edge of his sleeve. He felt cold, dirty and hungry. He cursed quietly to himself. After all those years of loyal service he had given the city, here he was, reduced to living like a hermit in a smelly, cramped, broken-down cow-shed on the edge of the Blean forest. "And all because of religion," he grumbled. It was a strange state of affairs when a man's conscience could be turned against him. Pride they called it. For him it had been a question of staying true to his beliefs or being like so many others, mouthing the right words at the right time for a quiet life. Still, on that score he had no regrets. The wheel would turn and perhaps then he could go back to his almshouse at St. Nicholas from which he and twelve other old men had been evicted two years before. That's if he lived long enough to see the false Queen, Mary the Catholic, overthrown or die and the English Church and faith restored.

Not that dissent against Popery was new. He remembered well, back in A.D. 1519, when he was eighteen years old, how impressed he had been to learn how the two reformers, Erasmus and Dean John Colet, had called at the Hospital at Harbledown and had refused to kiss the St. Thomas relic, the Holy Shoe Buckle. Dean Colet was reported to have said: "What, would this herd have us kiss the shoe of all good men! They must just as well offer their spittle to be kissed and other bodily excrements!" – or words to that effect, though less polite. That had made the young Giles think long and hard. But now such words would lead to imprisonment – or worse.

There was not much sign of happier days dawning soon. Mary had come to the throne two years before in A.D. 1553 and immediately the followers of the old Catholic faith had re-emerged and had begun to impose their beliefs and their wills upon the local folk requiring them to bow the knee and accept the Popish way of worship, saying to do otherwise was both heresy and treachery. So it was that when Giles and the fifty-nine other "brothers and sisters", as they were called, were ordered by the priest to attend Mass, he and twelve more brothers stood their ground, elderly as they were. They had humbly but firmly declined to comply. For this they had been expelled from the comfort and warmth of their almshouses, turned out into an uncaring world, labelled as malcontents and unless they kept out of sight and quiet, as heretics. So too for the ten sisters at St. John's hospital – and by the same canting priest. For two long, cold winters they had all suffered for their refusal to be bullied and forced to act against their consciences.

But Giles was a proud man and had seen much during his lifetime of the games of power played by the high and mighty. Back in the 1530s he had been working down in the city as a stone-mason and had witnessed the closure by King Henry of the St. Augustine's abbey, the nunnery and the friaries. "A lot of fine but cheap building-stone became available in those years," he remembered with a chuckle. And a lot of monks and nuns hurriedly moved away.

He recalled how in A.D. 1537 the City Council was taken over by stern Protestants, putting an end to the rich and corrupt idleness of many of the monks – or so they said. He remembered too, the day in December, A.D. 1539, when the traitorous John Stone was hung, drawn and quartered at the Don Johnne. He had not relished that prolonged and bloody act and had said as much to his young friend William Hopper.

"Some of these Protestant were as hard-minded and bigoted in their way as some of the Papists," he thought. "Most folk just want to be left alone to pray in their own way. Like me. Too much blood had been spilt, too many bones crushed, too many bodies burnt," he said to himself. "And all for what? It's not just the way we pray, but that this mad Queen is betrothed to the Spanish Philip. That is what *I* call treason." Tom Wyatt knew this and so had led a rising back in January at Rochester with four thousand men backing him. Wyatt entered London but had been surrounded, and surrendered. He, his allies Suffolk and Thomas Grey, Grey's daughters, the Lady Jane, and her husband, had all been beheaded. They had even kept the Princess Elizabeth close-confined, trying to trap her into confessing treason against her sister Mary. Giles had been told by a passing traveller the gates of London city and its main streets were festooned with gallows, each with a ripening corpse and as many as a hundred of Wyatt's followers had been executed in Kent. Now the terror had come to Canterbury.

It was a wet, chilly August morning, unseasonal with a blustery wind beating up the valley as Giles made his way down to the edge of the city. He crossed the river at the Ton-ford and made his way towards the wide Winne-cheape market-place. Here huddled groups of people stood around, talking quietly, many of them tight-faced. Today was special but with no cause for joy. In the distance a single bell began to toll, its slow clang, clang, clang marking death to come. The knots of bystanders moved together to form a silent crowd, heading slowly and almost reverently, it seemed to Giles, to the Burning Field. Here armed men with pikes formed a square, and there in the centre stood three stakes on a small mound, with piles of brushwood close to hand and a spluttering brazier tended by a young lad.

Giles gritted his teeth. To think, this would be where his friend William Hopper would die – and soon. And for what?

Months before, William alongside five others – Will Coker, Henry Lawrence, Dick Colliar, Richard Wright and Will Steve – had been arrested and held in the city prison. Here they had been badly beaten, ill-treated and half-starved, charged with heresy and treason. Eventually the group had been examined by Thornton, the Bishop of Dover, who found them guilty and condemned them to death. But execution had been deferred until the end of August. "An act of spite," thought Giles.

He was proud of his friend William. Word had got out that when first examined by Thornton he had seemed, in his dazed and battered state, to have granted the supremacy of the Catholic Church. But after resolving himself to a firmer state of mind, William had stuck to his personal truth which was to deny such. Although hectored and abused, he stood his ground – and on 16 July was finally sentenced to death at the stake.

Now, six weeks later, his real day of judgement had come.

Suddenly the crowd stirred. A slow procession was coming up the lane, led by a muffled drum. The six men were close-guarded, in chains, shuffling and stumbling. They were dressed in long, white smocks, their faces pale and gaunt but their eyes steadfast.

"These are brave men," thought Giles and a tear slid down his cheek. All around him women and men were sobbing or coughing to choke back their sorrow – or was it their anger?

Without any ceremony the six were shoved towards the three stakes, two to each. Quickly they were lashed tight and piles of brushwood and logs stacked around them, waist high, into one huge pyre. A black-cowled priest mumbled away in Latin, the drum rolled and suddenly there was silence. The priest then asked in a loud voice if any of the six wished now to recant. All six pulled themselves upright and replied in a firm voice, "No!"

With that the priest nodded to the beefy, masked executioner and his assistants. They each lit a torch from the brazier and plunged them into the pyre. A great sigh went up from the crowd and cries of: "God go with you!", "My brave boys!", "We are with you!" arose – and ceased almost immediately.

The damp brushwood spluttered and smoked but no flame took. More torches were thrust in.

"God, this will take forever," thought Giles, but then a gust of wind caught the flames and within seconds the pyre was burning furiously, sending great clouds of smoke and the acrid stench of burning flesh high into the sky. The dying men howled their anguish but it was soon over and then, as Giles lifted his head, a shaft of sunlight broke through, bathing the scene, causing a gasp amongst the crowd. "An omen," they said later. One day the light of truth will return.

Giles did not wait around for the clearing up – that was for ghouls. He had said farewell to his friend, he had witnessed his courage and fortitude. And now, as he plodded back uphill to his cow-shed home, he felt reassured, content almost, that this madness would pass and that he, in his own small way, together with his neighbours, had stood fast as free men of conscience whose day would come again.

Giles is an imagined character but his circumstances are based on real events. St. Nicholas' and St. John's almshouse dwellers were evicted for refusing "to bow the knee". William Hopper (a distant forebear of the author) and the others were burnt to death on what is now known as the Martyrs' Field, along with twenty-six other men and ten women in the years A.D. 1555-8. Five died in the Castle gaol.

The other characters and events are historically recorded. Queen Mary died in A.D. 1558, Elizabeth I came to the throne. Religious roles were reversed again but religious intolerance continued.

TALE FIFTEEN

For God and Our Rights

Three generations and a hundred years on the effects of the Reformation came to a head with the Civil War fought between Parliament and King Charles I. The roots of this dispute reached far back but were exacerbated by Queen Henrietta Maria's leanings towards Roman Catholicism at a time when Puritanism had taken a firm hold. With increases in printing, new ideas and reinterpretations of old ideas reached out amongst the commoners. There was another element, the emergence of a landed gentry, well-to-do men who, like their city merchant and professional contemporaries, resented the assumption of overweening superiority by members of the Court and the nobility. They wanted their share of power and prestige, a stronger voice in the running of the nation.

In Canterbury changes had happened, its population growing, helped by incoming Protestant Walloon and Hugenot refugees who brought with them new weaving skills, including those for silk. The city continued as a busy market town, with taverns, inns and workshops meeting the needs of the local rural community, a busy, bustling, brawling place. Out in the countryside, especially around Harbledown, apple, cherry and plum orchards were more dominant, as were, increasingly, the distinctive hop-gardens. But both the wooded Blean and Bigbury remained, much unchanged, commanding the skyline. The rural tranquillity was to be disrupted in A.D. 1642 as King and Parliament manoeuvred themselves into an inevitable collision course . . .

Richard felt mighty proud, although his inner conscience told him pride was a sin. Here he was, only seventeen years old but riding through his home village of Harbledown, well armed and mounted on a fine horse, one of Parliament's soldiers in Colonel Sandy's troop. They were on their way to secure for Parliament any weapons held in Canterbury. Although many in the city were good, upright Puritans, God-fearing Parliament folk, there were others, especially amongst those who ran the city's affairs, who were closet Royalists, King Charles' men. So far in these dangerous times they had kept their heads down, but they were not to be trusted, especially as it was rumoured Charles was about to raise his royal standard of defiance against Parliament at Nottingham.

The squabble between King and Parliament had been worsening now for several years, with the King and his Catholic Queen, Henrietta Maria, becoming more obstinate in their reactions. They were trying to impose their will over that of the people as well as squeezing them hard with unjust taxes. Well, that was how Richard saw it. The King was a weak and foolish man, wrongly advised by Popish courtiers and churchmen, edged into rash acts by his queen. Why, only back in January of this very year Charles had entered Parliament with armed men to try to arrest five of its members for treason, including Pym and Hampden. He found his prey had flown but the damage to his reputation was devastating. Charles had fled from the wrath of the citizens of London, as Richard knew only too well. He had been there, on the streets amongst the milling crowds of indignant protesters. It was then he signed up in one of the Training Bands, a militia unit.

Mind you, he had to add six months to his age to be accepted, but he was a tall, strong lad, already skilled at horse-riding and a good shot with the musket. His early years riding and hunting with his father in the Blean forests now held him in good stead. Richard was the second son of a fairly well-to-do master weaver who lived up a lane half a mile along the road from Harbledown village. Like many of his status and standing, his father was a staunch Puritan, conscious of his rights but who also knew well the powers of the local gentry and nobility. He often grumbled how the affairs of the city were run by such men, men whose understanding of God's will was . tempered by what that popish Archbishop Laud wanted. But the day of the Righteous was coming, he assured his family and neighbours.

Whilst Richard absorbed these ideas, he was more interested in what his grandfather, Richard Bridges, told him. Grandfather was for sure a godly man, but unlike many, neither a prude nor pious. He had little time, he told young Richard, for those who quoted the Lord's words and complained about the yoke inflicted on them by the King and the nobility but treated their own labourers and servants with unthinking harshness. "They may groan about the injustices they suffer, but forget the injustices they heap on others."

Richard was well aware of the poverty and disease suffered by the poor, not just in the surrounding villages but down in Canterbury's crowded, close-packed parishes, especially where the Walloon refugees were settled. He also knew of the savage penalties meted out for trivial offences, particularly by the Church courts. He had been told how a Robert Cushman had been punished for merely posting up a Puritan tract and missing church and how he had fled to the Low Countries for safety. Richard's own grandfather had had a narrow squeak back in the 1590s when as a young man he fell foul of some of the Harbledown worthies. They had brought him before the local justices for abusing the church-wardens, skipping in the morris dance and, perhaps what really upset them the most, for accusing a number of these substantial men of stealing timber from the local rough common wood. Grandfather always held that it was his exposure of their greedy thieving which got him into trouble, rather than telling the church-wardens they were demanding too much from the poor. "As for skipping in the morris dance, remember this. To be Godly does not stop a man or woman or child from being joyful. If some of these rich hypocrites spread a little more joy amongst the poor rather than blaming them for being poor, then surely God himself would smile. They act in a stiff-necked way, pretending all pleasure is a sin, then go home and beat the maid for their enjoyment."

So Richard grew to believe that the common folk were unjustly ill-used by those who claimed to be their betters but went to church regularly and spoke ponderously of God's will. These worthy folk wanted rights for themselves but were not always so keen on extending these rights to their humbler brethren. Even less, sharing any of their land and wealth. At fifteen, Richard, as the younger son, was sent off as an apprentice to his Uncle Jacques, a master weaver living close to Spitalfields in London, there to learn some of the new skills and styles coming in from the Low Countries. Once in London, Richard found himself caught up in the swirl of debate and discussion around the clash between the King and Parliament. He was exposed to new ideas, radical thoughts which crystallised into clarity many of the words of his grandfather about the rights of the common man. So when King Charles made his foolish and fateful decision to arrest the Five Members, Richard was ready to join one of the Training Bands. His skill and good sense quickly singled him out as a useful recruit. The militia were trained

99

by professional soldiers and soon Richard had learned how to handle a broad-sword as well as a pistol, whilst his riding ability made him particularly valued. That is why he was posted to Colonel Sandy's troop, under the command of Sir Michael Livesey, when Parliament decided to seize the arsenals in Kent. His local knowledge of Canterbury and East Kent would likely be put to good use.

In the course of five days Sir Michael's men had fanned out across the county, taking Rochester castle without a fight. Many great houses, the homes of known Royalist sympathisers, were searched for arms, armour and gunpowder and in the process valuable goods and money had been 'liberated'. At Rochester cathedral Richard witnessed something which made him feel uneasy. Some of the more strict-minded of the troopers, encouraged by their commander, himself a stern Puritan, interrupted a service and proceeded to destroy the fine-carved altar-rails and other furnishings they deemed as "ungodly". Richard could understand such trappings were a diversion in God's house but recognised the skill and effort that must have gone into the intricate carving, the fine woodworking and cloth weaving of what was destroyed.

"These things could have been found a home elsewhere," he thought. "Honest men and women had laboured hard and long to create them. Now they were destroyed at the blow of an axe."

He remembered this incident as the mounted troop jogged towards Harbledown. It was a grey, sultry August day, overcast, breezeless, hot and humid. Sweat trickled down under his thick, buff leather riding-coat. He and his fellow troopers had yet to be issued with breast and back-plates, although each had been given a pot-shaped helmet which weighed hot and heavy. They had made good speed from Sittingbourne that day but now horses and men alike were tiring in the oppressive heat. As they rode, Captain Baynes had signalled Richard to come up beside him to tell what he knew of the villages and big houses hereabouts. Richard waved towards the lane running up to his father's house. "You won't be finding anything up there, sir," he said, "for that's where my family lives, nor much else this side of the city. The village ahead is Harbledown, with two old churches. One is given over to the poor and sick. There is no cluttering of ungodly baubles there. The other, St. Michael's, is plain and also true. The preacher there is Richard Culmer, an upright, forthright and downright righteous man who will likely meet us in Canterbury." He forebore to tell the Captain how disliked Culmer was by many of the local folk.

To Richard's relief the Captain indicated they would not bother to look the two churches over. They were to ride straight on into Canterbury. As they entered through the Westgate they were generally well received; mostly, Richard noticed, by the ordinary townspeople. With the help of preacher Culmer, who was indeed waiting to meet up with them, together with the less enthusiastic Mayor and Sheriffs, the few weapons kept at the Westgate were impounded and a guard set. The rest of the troop made their way through the narrow streets to the Cathedral gates to take into custody the two loads of arms and six barrels of gunpowder held by the Dean. Gazing up at the statue of Christ, filling a large niche in the ornamental stonework above the archway, Captain Baynes put on a grim face. "This is idolatry at its worst. This must not be. Bad enough all that stained glass windowing and those heathen faces carved in the stonework. It must come down!"

The hard men in the troop needed no further urging. Some had already primed their muskets and within minutes a hail of shots was shattering the stone edifice, spattering chunks in all directions. Richard did not join in, but sat gentling his horse, feeling uneasy as he had at Rochester three days before. A large crowd had gathered, some of them cheering, but Richard noticed a large number stood tight-faced, unsmiling.

"This is not a wise thing to do," he thought. "We should be winning these people over to our just cause, not destroying with glee, even if it be idolatrous." His unease grew greater when some of the troopers marched into the Cathedral itself, even taking their horses with them. This time they contented themselves with smashing ancient coloured glass windows. Richard remembered these from early childhood, how his grandfather had stood him to catch the glowing colours as the sun streamed in, reds, golds, greens, blues. "See the beauty of God's colours my boy. Take no notice of the pictures, skilled as they are. The real purity is in the light and the colours, God's joy." And now they were mere shards of broken glass, lifeless and dull underfoot.

That night Richard got permission to ride out to visit his family. They were surprised and delighted to see him, not knowing he had been doing Parliament's work. He sat and talked long into the night with his father and grandfather, the three of them trying to grasp the magnitude of what was happening, whether there would now be a civil war and what might happen when the King lost, as lose he must. Among other things they told him how Preacher Culmer had upset even more local people, ranting against drunkeness from the pulpit, naming names, and sending his sons to spy on those who dared to play cricket on the Sabbath even though it was in a field up near the woods. His sons had been driven off with a hail of stones.

"Such men as Culmer are no help to the great cause," said grandfather. "The issues are too important to be blurred by such over-righteous zealots. Things must change in this land and rights be given to the common folk," he continued. "It will not serve us well to replace one tyrant with a new set of overlords who are interested only in preserving their wealth, their lands, their power. It must go further." Richard's father looked uneasy at these words. He had long tolerated the old man's views but even for him, however displeased with his own status he might be, such ideas appeared to be going too far.

But Richard never forgot those words. In the coming months, as the Civil War developed from skirmish and ambush into full-scale battles, every time he charged with the cry of "For God and our rights!" the image of his grandfather flicked into his mind. "Our rights!" he remembered.

Six years later, now twenty-three years old, Richard had fought back and forth across England, at Marston Moor, at Naseby. He was now back in Canterbury, under General Fairfax, part of an army sent to take the city, fortunately peacefully. The cause of the trouble had been the joyless bigotry of the Puritan Mayor who had foolishly banned Christmas celebrations. This had led to riots and triggered off a rising against Parliament across Kent. Richard thought the Second Civil War was a sad mistake brought about by the same stiff-necked obstinacy his grandfather had warned against.

The riots had brought retribution on the city, more unthinking destruction. The city gates were burned, part of the city walls pulled down and, when the rioters were put on trial in April 1648, the jurors refused to convict them. It was clear then where local sympathies lay. The gentry rose against Parliament and many followed them. After a hard and bloody fight through the streets of Maidstone, Fairfax's army came to Canterbury and there, at the Cathedral, received the surrender of a mountain of weapons and three hundred horses. This time the Archbishop's Palace was looted and destroyed.

It was during this return visit to Canterbury that Richard learned more of the damage wrought by Preacher Culmer, or "Blue Dick" as he was now called. Richard spent some time wandering around the Cathedral, noting with growing dismay the damage done, although he dared not make comment. It turned out that back in 1643 Culmer had been appointed by authority of Parliament to detect and cause to be demolished the superstitious inscriptions and idolatrous monuments in the Cathedral. And he had, leading a three day assault of smashing and breaking and pulling down whatever he considered objectionable, which was much. Richard shook his head sadly for this was not what he had fought for.

A year later, in A.D. 1649, the Civil War was over. The King had been captured, tried and beheaded and a Commonwealth proclaimed. Parliament now ruled the land although there were many, including Richard, who thought there were still too many Lords and gentry-folk in office. Richard had by this time become one of the Levellers, a strong group within the army who held that all men were equal before God. This being so, they should be equal before the law. They wanted the right to vote to be extended, freedom of religious belief not just one conformity; they demanded liberty of conscience, the end of press censorship and the breaking of Church power. Richard had been at the great debates at Putney the year before, when delegates from all parts of Parliament's victorious New Model Army had met with Fairfax and other army leaders, including Oliver Cromwell, to hammer out an Agreement. But it had fallen through, not least, as Richard saw it, because the men of power wanted to keep their power, not share it.

By now, he had had enough of fighting and traipsing up and down the land. When the chance came to stand down he took it and rode home. Not for him fighting in Ireland, butchering and burning women and children in the name of God. Meantime, he was still young, life was to be lived and enjoyed. He married into a respected local Walloon family and in time became a successful cloth-merchant, a kindly, considerate master but one who kept his deepest beliefs much to himself, passing them on to his three sons. The youngest of these, John, emigrated to the New World, settling in what became Boston, setting up as a merchant trader. It would have given Richard, and his grandfather, much joy to know that one day one of Richard's great-grandsons would fight against the English king's armies in the American War of Independence and that he too would charge with the cry of "For God and our rights!" on his lips. And would win.

Richard is fiction, the other characters real, including grandfather Bridges. The main events and incidents concerning Culmer are recorded.

Both St. Nicholas' and St. Michael's churches appear to have escaped damage during the Civil War. Puritanism continued to have a stronghold in the city and surrounding countryside but Canterbury gave a joyous welcome to Charles II when he arrived in May 1660. The ideas and spirit of the Levellers lived on, suppressed but potent.

TALE SIXTEEN

The Turn-pike

In the years after the Civil War trade and farming flourished, with new wealth beginning to pour in as maritime power and commerce reached even further across the oceans. Canterbury consolidated as a centre for weaving fine silk and other cloth, new houses were built, old ones embellished, whilst the markets and mills stayed busy. The rich did well but the poor still died young. At Harbledown little changed other than a marked increase in hop-gardens, now spreading across the rolling farmland towards Bigbury, intermingled with orchards. Bigbury itself remained unaltered, a dark hump of trees on the skyline. To outward appearances Harbledown had a prosperous and tranquil landscape supporting a comfortable livelihood but not for all. Life for the landless farm labourer and his family was hard, especially when misfortune struck. Then you turned to the Parish for help . . .

The gang of labourers mending the road were a sorry looking lot. A dozen in number, they worked slowly and miserably in the pouring rain, water dripping from their improvised sacking head-coverings, their well-worn clothing mud-spattered. It was one of those cold, wet, grey November days, with the clouds lying low over the Blean woods and Bigbury. The trees were bare and piles of fallen leaves drifted onto the road, making the ground slippery underfoot.

The labourers were an assorted bunch, mainly young lads and old men, mostly on Parish Poor relief, made to do the Parish work of keeping the road repaired. This was the old main road to London, used since Roman times, but the responsibility of the Parish to keep in good order where it ran through Harbledown. So four times a year, whatever the weather, the workforce was assembled, given picks and shovels and a couple of cart loads of flints and pebbles, and set to work, filling in potholes and ruts, cleaning back weeds and grass, firming up the edges and digging out the roadside ditches. It was hard work, not made any easier by the continual flow of carts, wagons, horses and the occasional coach splashing by. It was a dangerous place to be for some drivers still took the bend at the bottom of the hill by St. Nicholas' church too fast, skidding and sliding and more than one fully laden cart had tipped over that year, blocking the road, much to the delight of the village children.

There were other times when the road became impassable, when blocked with ice and snow, drifting in on the strong north-easterlies. So out again went a gang of labourers, the Parish poor, set to clear a way through for the London to Dover coaches. The Parish officers took much pride in the speed with which the snow was shovelled away, as if it were they who toiled, freezing and wet, rather than the unfortunates forced through poverty to do their bidding. One such poor man was George, now in his mid-fifties, a gnarled, weather-beaten man who had virtually lived his whole life in Harbledown, working hereabouts as a wood-cutter, farm labourer, drover and general handyman. Like many others, he used to make the annual visit to the Canterbury Michaelmas Hiring Fair, there to stand with the great throng of men and women who were seeking work, either on the farms or within the city. Some saw it as a sort of human cattle market, with the human beasts being sized for strength and stamina – and in certain cases for beauty or handsome looks.

Once the contract was fixed, then you were no longer free. Woe betide any who skipped off and were caught by the law. There were those who grumbled it was not right that any man, or even woman perhaps, would be bound to one master or mistress, at their beck and call without redress for insult, injury or illness. Some masters were fair-minded, others not so, but in these hard times work was work. The alternative, being on the Parish, or wandering the countryside, didn't bear thinking about. There were some who slipped off to Sheerness to become sailors, no questions asked. Others made the long trek to London town, to be swallowed up by the great city. And of course there were those like the men near the coast and up in the woods who took to smuggling and thieving, even daring to halt and rob the coaches as they toiled up the hill from Boughton, their horses flagging and easy to stop. But the local justices were quick to pounce and deal harshly with any such wrong-doers, if they were caught.

In some ways, as a single man, life was not so hard for George in his earlier years. The pressure on the married men with a wife and children was great for if they fell foul of their master they would be evicted, sent packing with whatever possessions they could carry. Desolate, miserable family groups pushing a handcart laden with their few household goods were not an uncommon sight on the road, forced to camp out under hedges, begging for food, seeking employment, if only for a few pence or a dry barn to sleep in. For many generations now the Parish register at St. Michael's showed, for any who cared to read or could read, that scarcely a year went by without the death of a still-born infant or lone wayfarer being recorded, often as not, unnamed.

Being single, George could fit in easily, taking up little space, usually in an outhouse or shed or in a small attic room over the farm-kitchen or stables. A quiet man, he had little learning and like all the other hired-hands attended St. Michael's church each Sunday, sitting at the back whilst the gentry occupied the front pews. He had, however, a quick mind and would often think over what the Rector had said in his sermon and contrast it with words he heard read out in the lessons. Ideas like "Love thy neighbour as thyself", "The meek shall inherit the earth", "Do unto others, as you would have them do unto you" sounded fine but why did so few of the upright masters and mistresses practice what their Rector preached? Or were they just hypocrites, showing generosity only on public occasions such as the Harvest Home and Christmas when all could see what fine charitable Christian folk they were?

George had been on his own since the age of fourteen, when both his parents died, swept off by the plague they had contracted from mingling with the crowds down at the market in Canterbury. Fortunately, George had been able to stay on with their farmer employer, but only on sufferance until the harvest was in. Then he was down to Canterbury to hire out his labour and found work as a pot-boy in one of the city's busy ale-houses. Canterbury at this time was a thriving market town, a stopping off place for travellers journeying to and from Dover and a centre for silk weaving, brought by incomers from France. George did not like his work, fetching and carrying jugs of beer for drunken, foul-mouthed men and women, cleaning up their vomit, ducking their fists, ignoring their abuse. And after working late he was forced to sleep in a flea-infested garret up under the roof, fed only on scraps and left-overs. The inn was down near the river, damp and unhealthy and as soon as his time was served he was off and away, feeling himself lucky to find work minding sheep, a lonely but pleasanter task.

As the seasons rolled by and the years passed George worked his way through most farming jobs, picking up skills and knowledge, becoming adept at caring for and handling sheep and cattle, ploughing, sowing, and reaping, planting and pruning fruit trees, digging ditches, mending fences but above all else he loved working with hops. In autumn and winter there was hand-digging the hop-gardens, preparing the ground, then erecting the twelve to sixteen feet high chestnut poles, exactly spaced out in rows, followed by the pruning of the old vines. Then came the weeding and the anxious watching in the spring for the first thin twining stems to appear and, with some helpful training, see them rapidly start up the poles. If all went well, by midsummer, he would walk through the avenues of massed greenery looking for the tell-tale yellow flowers. These were worrying times, waiting for the green-yellow hop-cones to ripen, a time summed up by the old saying: "First the flea and then the fly. Then the mould and then they die." But if all went well, in late-summer and early-autumn, came the hop-picking when men, women and children came out from the city to help. A cheerful, bustling time it was, full of laughter and banter as the poles were uprooted and the bines brought down, ready for stripping. The Harbledown hop-gardens extended over the gently undulating slopes towards Bigbury hill, a rolling sea of green whose beauty often caused comment from passing travellers.

At these times George preferred to be in the open air with all the cheerful folk, though the hours were long and the work dirty. It was better than being cooped up inside for the hop-drying; now that was hot, tiring and painstaking labour, although he liked filling the dried hops into the hop-pockets, great sacks which smelt as only hops could. He always filled his pillow with the soft, rustling hop heads and swore that was what kept winter coughs and colds away. He also enjoyed the annual Hopkin feast, the hop-harvest supper at the end of the hop-picking, with its music and dancing, the casks of beer and overflowing tables and, always, the huffkins, the unsweetened cakes made specially for this celebration. But for him those days had gone.

Two years past George had been forced to throw himself on the mercy of the Parish. A wagon wheel had run over his foot, breaking several bones which had set badly. He was unable to work for weeks and when he had recovered could now only walk with a limp. So he was of no use to his employer, a curt, hard man who dismissed him and turned him out. Not a Christian thing to do, thought George, but not unexpected. Fortunately, George was well known in the Parish so when he went to ask for help he was, albeit grudgingly he thought, found a home in an unused wood-cutter's shed up near the common, an act of grace and favour on the part of the local squire. Here he set up house, acquiring a few sticks of furniture from kind-hearted folk he knew, making the rest for himself using his carpenter skills. He received a weekly payment from the Parish, just enough to buy food and a few other necessities but in exchange he would have to turn out when needed to help mend the road, working the best he could with his lame leg.

George did not mind this arrangement for he knew that as an aging part-cripple he would never be employed again, nor was there any family or kin to take him in. He would have to rely on the Parish at least to keep him alive, if not in comfort. He took to wiling away the lonely hours carving small animals, birds and figures which he gave to his friends' children. They came to visit, sometimes bringing an egg or two, a punnet of berries, a few vegetables or even the left over remains of rabbit stew. Over the years George himself had learned how to set simple traps, and on moonless nights he would silently slip out of his shed-cottage for a spot of poaching. But this was a risky business for the local landowners set man-traps, fearsome, snapping, sharp-toothed horrors that could take off a man's leg. George was careful and quiet, keeping to fields and copses he knew well.

He rarely ventured into Canterbury, finding the walk back uphill painful and tiring. The city itself was too crowded for his liking, with people pushing and shoving, busy about their business, with carts, horses and coaches trundling through the narrow, overhung streets. Worst of all were the town boys who jeered at the limping, poorly clad man, throwing mud and stones at him, taunting him to give chase. So as far as possible he stayed away.

And here he was, helping mend the road, told by a church-warden several days before to be down by St. Nicholas' church at dawn on this raw November Thursday in A.D. 1729. He did his best to help, set the task of sorting stones and flints from the great heap tipped out of the carts. Big, small and middle-sized. As they worked the men talked, the usual gossip about who had got drunk, who had beaten his wife, who was the likely father of young Alice's child, how much money the squire had lost at gambling. From time to time odd bits of real news emerged. How it now seemed there would be no war with Spain since Walpole's treaty, what massive fortunes were being made by the traders going to the East Indies, and the growing prosperity of Bristol and other ports from the slave-trading from Africa to the Americas. Then there was talk of the latest exploits of the North Kent Gang, the smugglers who worked out of Herne Bay and Thanet.

There was one piece of news that caused George to smile: "This 'ere bit o'road is te be taken over by one o'theym Turn-pike Trusts next year, so's I 'ear," said one of the labourers. "I 'eard it doun in Cant-a-bury. Theym locul nobs 'ave got agether for a Parliament'ry hact, theym call it. What that'um mean is theym teck o'er runnin the road, meck it good and charge a price for journey'in on it. Theyms puts up gates, toll gates, with'm man who tecks money and opens up, an' on you go."

"Wull," replied another, "theym no makin' me pay t'travul on t'King's highway. We's al know ways doun int' Cant-a-bury an' o'er t'Fevurs-ham wi'out walkin' thisa road." He spat decisively. "No me. No t'Toll tax and that's a final!"

The others voiced their agreement and the talking turned to other things. But George was puzzled. If the local gentry were banding together to take over the road and keep it in good order, who was going to do the work he and his fellows were now doing? They wouldn't want to hire men for just a few days a year to fill potholes and shift snow. The question was left unanswered as he bent down again to his stone-sorting.

A year later George knew the answer to the puzzle for he was back, doing the same tasks, this time supervised by one of the local Trust-owners, a silly, loud-voiced man who kept urging them to talk less and work harder. It had turned out turn-piking of the road had not relieved the Parish of its duty to provide labourers to mend it. So, as George worked it out, the only difference was that the same men who ran the Parish now owned the Turn-pike but made a profit from their tolls. And it was the same poor men who did the repair work, still for no pay.

"So we are working for them, for nothing except our little bit of Poor Relief. That is how the rich get richer and we poor stay poor," thought George bitterly, bending to shift more stones for yet another pothole.

George is an imagined character but the events and agricultural, economic and social backgrounds are well documented. Whilst the Turn-pike Trusts led to an improvement in the road and transport system, helping trade and commerce and the development of a speedier coach service, there was a hidden cost paid by the Parish poor.

TALE SEVENTEEN

Grace's Story

Rural poverty remained a characteristic throughout the 18th century and on into the 19th century, not helped by a growing population and changes in farming technique requiring less labour. Trade continued to flourish and the industrial revolution began affecting and diminishing the demand for the products made by Canterbury's weavers but other industries like brewing and leather making expanded within the city. The French Revolution and the Napoleonic Wars left an imprint on the city with the building of barracks and fine houses for the officers and their families, as well as humbler dwellings for their servants. A huge one hundred feet high mill, Denne's Mill, helped dominate the city skyline along with the Cathedral. The development of the coaching trade coincided with the network of improved turn-pike roads, leading to the demolition of all the city's gates except the Westgate. A railway link to Whitstable was built in 1830, a wonder of the new age.

Outside the city at Harbledown hop-gardens spread all around, new cottages had been built close to St. Nicholas' church whilst Upper Harbledown began to emerge as a street village along the main road. Up towards the Blean woods ancient common land was enclosed and smallholdings began to appear. But all was not well . . .

Grace hitched up her skirts and ran nimbly down the muddy lane. In the distance she could hear a buzz of voices and an occasional loud, jeering laugh. There they were, a large crowd of men, women and children, some local, most up from Canterbury. Here, where the London road wound its way into Harbledown all these folk had come to meet HIM, Sir William, though some disrespectfully called him "Mad Tom". She hadn't seen so many people gathered together since the opening of the Canterbury to Whitstable railway when she was twelve years old, in May

1830 that was. Then she and her whole family, with folk from all around, had walked over to the tunnel to see the carriages and wagons being hauled uphill from Canterbury. It had been a grand sight.

Now it was the afternoon of Friday 12 April 1833, a windy, fresh Spring day, with clouds racing in over Bigbury. The ground underfoot was wet and claggy but this didn't dampen the crowd's spirit. Grace edged into the throng. She was a small, stocky, fair-haired fifteen-year-old who until two years ago lived with her parents and three sisters and a brother in a small, crowded cottage, close by St. Nicholas' churchyard. At thirteen she had gone into service with a farmer and his wife a few miles away at Boughton-under-Blean. The wife was a boney, sharp-faced woman, meek and humble in the presence of her betters but a real harridan harpy, shouting at her children, nagging Grace and hectoring her neighbours over imagined slights. He was tall, dark-haired, pious and pompous but like his wife given to lying and deceit when it suited. Both were tight-fisted. Grace often had to bite her lip and keep her natural spirit well hidden. She had no choice. Her father was a poor farm labourer and the family lived on the edge of poverty, as did so many others. Times were hard and Grace's few shillings a year helped keep the family going.

Such was the degree of rural desperation that ever since 1830 throughout the local countryside and all across most of southern and central England many farmworkers had been expressing their rage at their continued poverty and degradation. New machinery was replacing honest labourers and throwing them out of work. The disturbances were all led by the mysterious Captain Swing, who was everywhere and nowhere.

Grace often recalled how on her thirteenth birthday, October 8 1830, the whole family had turned out to watch a red glow in the sky up over Blean. "That'll be Captain Swing at work," chuckled her father. "He's been busy again." Just two months before the local countryside had erupted with the smashing of a new threshing machine at Lower Hardres, a few miles to the southeast across the Stour valley. News filtered through over the following weeks of similar happenings, including rick and barn burning across the county, from Orpington to Newington and, more locally, at Barton and Boughton Hill. Grace was especially pleased by the destruction of that barn, owned by her mean-minded master.

In the following weeks and months Captain Swing struck again and again, at Upstreet, Bekesbourne, Rainham, Selling Court, Hollingbourne, again and again at Boughton Hill, at Herne Hill, over at Wingham, Eastry, Birchington and many other places. The whole countryside seethed with rumours and insurrection but it was a secret army that attacked and always at night, putting fear and dread into the local rich farmers, landowners and gentry. They still remembered the French Revolution, just a generation before. Grace recalled her grandfather telling her of the wars with the French. "They may have been Froggies but they knew what to do with their King," he would say. "Just like we did back awhile." But just like before, the King's men eventually suppressed the riots, with a few hangings, a large number of transportations to the penal colonies and many more given jail sentences.

The distress in the countryside had not ended and now there was a new player on the scene in East Kent, Sir William Courtenay. "Perhaps things will change, perhaps Sir William will lead us forward to the promised land," thought Grace. It had been just a few weeks before, over at the Three Squirrels inn at Boughton, when Grace and her young farm labourer friend, George Griggs, had stood on tiptoe at the window, listening to the great man's powerful voice promising a new land of freedom and plenty to those who followed him. They had been most impressed. Now he was coming to Harbledown.

But who was this Sir William? He had appeared at Canterbury a few months before, in September 1832, immediately attracting attention with his long, black hair and beard and his flamboyant clothing. An imposing man, he was thirty-three years old, nearly six feet tall, broad-shouldered and barrel-chested with strong arms. His eyes were light-blue and strangely brilliant. First he claimed to be Count Moses Rothschild, though some said his real name was John Tom. He quickly became known as a local figure, strolling the streets of Canterbury, frequenting the local societies, clubs and public houses. Then, suddenly, after a few weeks he announced he was really Sir William Courtenay, Knight of Malta and the rightful heir to the Earldom of Devon. He made such an impression that in December he was asked by some disaffected local Tories to stand for election to Parliament. Which he did, as an Independent to embarrass the otherwise unopposed Hon. Richard Watson and Lord Fordwich. This was to be the first election after the passing of the Reform Bill which gave the vote to more men, but only men of property or financial means.

He conducted his campaign from the Rose Inn, at the corner of Rose Lane, and from here he drove through the streets in a barouche,

113

extravagantly dressed, making wild and populist speeches, promising all things to all men. To no avail. In spite of generating fierce loyalty and much excitement he lost badly to Watson and Fordwich.

Straightaway he again stood for election, this time for East Kent, attracting huge crowds at the race course on Barham Downs, but in the end received only three votes and much derision.

He bounced back quickly. Over the coming months he toured the local villages, addressing meetings all over East Kent, publishing his own newspaper, *The Lion*, but eventually his luck ran out and he was brought to trial for perjury and swindling on 29 March 1833. By now he had gathered a huge local following who milled around the Westgate city gaol for hours after he had been lodged there, threatening to free him. Troops were brought in from Dover to protect the Mayor and Corporation from the angry mob.

He was released on 8 April and allowed to leave for London to seek bail at the Court of the King's Bench. And now he was returning, due to arrive here at Harbledown this very afternoon.

Grace did not have to wait long for over the hill and round the bend came a small procession of men on horseback, other humbler folk following on foot. The crowd erupted with cheers. Sir William was back. Caught up in the jostling, excited mass Grace glimpsed a sight of her friend, George Griggs. He had walked all the way from Boughton to be close to his hero. They edged towards each other, smiled and linked hands. Together they followed the jubilant procession down into Canterbury, marching behind two banners, one proclaiming: "Truth bears off the Victory", the other: "The British Lion shall be Free." Sir William received a hero's welcome that day in the city, a day Grace would never forget. There was a special place in her heart for this fine figure of a man – and perhaps also for George.

Five years later Grace was trudging up the long, straight road past the scattered farms and cottages later known as Upper Harbledown, towards Dunkirk, the small, neglected, church-less and school-less village high on the Blean plateau. She was on her way back to Boughton from a visit to her parents in Harbledown. Dunkirk had a reputation for lawlessness and around abouts the local folk were known for their fierce sense of independence.

"They be all smugglers and thieves up there," her mother told her. "Don't you give any o' 'em time o'day, my girl."

Every so often a coach or carriage clattered by, the horses snorting with exertion. Horsemen, light carts and wagons passed her for this was the main road from London to Dover. Grace walked on paying no mind as she was determined to get to Dunkirk by seven o'clock this Sunday evening, 27 May 1838, for HE was to speak to the assembled believers. George would be there too for even now discontent rumbled amongst the rural poor.

Grace's father had explained to her why so many folk felt bitter. The government had ended the old system of helping the poor and workless by giving them money from the Parish according to the number of their children, called "Outdoor Relief", and put in its place a new scheme whereby there were harsh means tests and the threat of big, new, bleak workhouses to put people off seeking help. "They want us to starve quietly or grovel for help," he said. "You mark my words, girl. They'll try to break our spirit as well as our bodies." But down in Canterbury the City fathers had refused to co-operate with the London-based Poor Law Commission, as had Dover, Margate and Ramsgate. All had refused to join the local government-sponsored Poor Law Unions, which grouped Parishes together. Not so in nearby Faversham, where the local gentry wasted no time and set up their Poor Law Union with alacrity, pressing ahead with cutting the relief and making up half the payment with a bread ticket. They should have known better, and back in 1835 Grace, who was still a live-in house servant at Boughton, witnessed the flickering embers of countryside revolt against poverty fanned into flame again by the stupidity of the Faversham Poor Law Guardians. In their haste to impose the new ways they set off a chain of demonstrations across the Swale area. In village after village there were noisy protests, threats and scuffles. In Canterbury the City fathers watched anxiously, glad they had read the signs and held back on implementing this new scheme, whilst out in the villages like Harbledown, folk waited for news from up the road.

Grace saw one of the protests over at Boughton on Tuesday 5 May 1855, when a small crowd of about forty men and women marched down to the village, led by a man carrying a flag. They were seeking the cart carrying bread for paupers with the intention of breaking it up. This time it came to nothing, but on that same day, over at Lynsted, a strong body of determined men and women had prevented the hated bread tickets being issued. But within two days this latest standing together of farmworkers had been put down at Rodsmersham. Here the local gentry laid a trap, bringing in Metropolitan policemen from London, the 28th

Foot from Chatham and two hundred Special Constables, mostly farmers and townsmen from Faversham. The crowd thought they had won when they chased off the Poor Law Union officials, but ran straight into the soldiers of the 28th Foot. The demonstrators fled in all directions but only twenty were captured. Altogether thirty-nine were brought to trial in Canterbury, most receiving jail sentences of three months or more. Most of those who took part escaped, some to live to fight another day.

That was three years ago and by now Grace was a full-grown woman of twenty, still in service with the same miserable master and mistress but saving every halfpenny so that she could marry George Griggs. He had remained slight and wiry in build and was counted as an experienced farmworker, but one in whom a sense of injustice still rankled. He, like Grace, continued to have faith in their hero, Sir William, and remembered well that April day when he returned in triumph from London. In their eyes he had been betrayed for within weeks he had been tried for perjury at the Assizes at Maidstone, found guilty, sentenced to three months' imprisonment and seven years' transportation. But worse was to follow. His wife, a Mrs. Tom and several relations from Truro tracked him down and by October had managed to have him certified as a lunatic and transferred from prison to the Barming Heath asylum. They said his real name was John Nicholls Tom, the rest a wheeling fantasy. But the two young people never really believed their hero was other than a great man, come to deliver them, as he had promised. And now he was back with them.

Sir William, as they loyally called him, had stayed at the Barming Heath asylum until October 1837 when he was released into the care of his old friend Mr. Francis, of Fairbrook, Boughton-under-Blean. As it turned out, a place and a time well suited to his messianic talents, a powder keg waiting for the spark. There was an air of sullen resentment lurking close to the surface and Sir William, on his walkabouts, soon became aware that this was fertile ground for his talents. He still kept up the pretence he was the rightful Earl of Devon, convincing his host, Mr. Francis, that gaining his rightful inheritance was his sole objective, but all the time he was working his way into the confidence of local farmers and smallholders, as well as the farmworkers and their families, especially through their children. He again took to wearing extravagant clothes and began carrying a brace of pistols.

In the end, in January 1838, Francis threw him out, upset and angry at the betrayal, as he saw it, of his trust and generosity. Unperturbed, Sir

William rode off and spent the next few months touring East Kent, holding court, living well off the hospitality of others, impressing the locals, speaking out against the Poor Law, building a strong base of support. In Herne Hill and Boughton he was held almost in reverence, especially by the Culver family of Bossenden Farm, close to Dunkirk. Particularly Sarah Culver, unmarried, forty-years-old and flattered by his attentions. His mania took on a new twist for he began to speak of himself as the reincarnation of Jesus Christ, the Saviour, come to lead his flock to a new and better world. There were those, in their desperation and ignorance, who believed, or half-believed him.

So it was then, on this warm Sunday evening, some two hundred people gathered to meet with him at Dunkirk, Grace and George amongst them. After reading from the Bible Sir William spoke passionately about the wrong-doings of the rich, the injustices heaped upon the poor, the iniquities of the Poor Law. This was well received and Sir William left to loud acclamation but not before telling them to be ready on the coming Tuesday to follow him in a great cause.

Tuesday came. Sir William met up with a handful of followers, including George, and proceeded to lead them on a tour of the local countryside, gathering up men as he went, ending up back at Bossenden Farm. Early the next morning they were off once more, Sir William resplendent in a broad-brimmed hat and smock, with a brace of pistols and a sword. They marched all the way to Sittingbourne, then swung south back through the villages to Bossenden Farm again. But none joined them. Meanwhile the local landowners were in a high state of agitation and early on the following morning of Thursday 31 May, John Mears, the High Constable of Boughton-under-Blean, a plumber by trade, went with his brother Nicholas and his assistant Daniel Edwards, with a warrant to arrest Sir William and his chief followers at Bossenden Farm.

It ended in tragedy. When confronted Sir William exploded with rage, shot and stabbed Nicholas Mears and had his body thrown in a ditch. The two others fled in panic. The news of this violent murder spread rapidly. Grace heard of it from a passer-by as she was feeding the chickens later that morning. Fear struck through her for she knew George was with Sir William and would therefore be deeply implicated in the killing. Meanwhile, Sir William bullied and harangued his band of followers to stay firm in their belief in him and marched them off to Fairbrook House. No sooner had they arrived than someone spotted soldiers coming up the road. They had marched from Canterbury in answer to the urgent pleas of the local Justice of the Peace. Also now on the scene was Norton Knatchbull, a local magistrate, with a mixed band of constables and local gentry. After a brief but noisy stand-off and an exchange of badly aimed pistol shots, Sir William led his men away across the fields towards Bossenden Woods. Knatchbull rode off and set up his headquarters at the Red Lion inn on Watling Street at Dunkirk. It was here, early in the afternoon, that Grace, breathless with running uphill, joined a clamouring, restless crowd of men, women and children. The soldiers stood at ease. The minutes ticked by. It was a hot, sultry day, with storm clouds brewing high in the sky.

Word came from Knatchbull's scouts. Sir William and his men had halted in a small clearing not far from the footpath from Old Barn Lane. The order was given for the troops to move into the woods. At that moment a tremendous thunderstorm broke, with torrential rain. Grace pushed her way into a corner of the Red Lion, now packed with the excited crowd. There was nothing to do but wait, wait and pray.

Out in the woods it was soon over. The troops, under the direction of a Major Armstrong, split into two prongs, one with a Captain Reed, the other with Lieutenant Bennett and Norton Knatchbull. Bennett and his twenty-five men moved in on Sir William and his thirty-five followers, most armed merely with stout clubs and staves. Only one, other than Sir William, had a firearm. It was now about 3 p.m. The rain stopped. The only sound was of soldiers' boots crashing through the wet, steamy undergrowth.

Sir William saw Bennett and his men approaching and led a disorganised charge, pistolling the young Lieutenant dead with one shot. At that moment Armstrong arrived and ordered his men to open fire. A volley cracked out, men fell and the two groups closed together, musket butts, clubs, fists and boots flailing. It took only three to four minutes of frenzied hand to hand fighting before in a small trampled space some twenty dead or wounded men lay scattered about, including the riddled body of Sir William. But his followers fought on until Armstrong ordered a bayonet charge. It was enough. They broke and fled. One of those shot was George Griggs, hit in the stomach by a musket ball, groaning and dying in a ditch as he tried to hold in his spilling intestines with both hands.

Altogether eight men were dead, including Sir William, seven other wounded, one to die later. As well as Bennett, a Faversham special constable called Catt was killed, caught by a round from his own side. So ended the "Battle of Bossenden Wood", as it became called.

Back at the Red Lion, Grace and the others heard the crackle of musket fire, the shouts and screams. Then silence. The crowd trooped outside and waited, now nervous and pale-faced. Not for long, for out of the woods came a slow procession, bearing the bodies. The battered and bloodied remains were laid out on the stable floor for all to see. Grace recognized George, pushed her way through the crowd and fell to the ground, grasping for his hand. She was quickly bundled away and was left weeping in a corner, weeping for what was and for what might have been. Her two heroes lay dead, side by side.

George Griggs lies buried in the churchyard at Boughton-under-Blean, Sir William Courtenay and eight of his followers were all buried in Hernehill churchyard and are commemorated by a plaque. Lieutenant Bennett was buried in the Cathedral cloisters and is commemorated by a tablet on the north wall of the nave. Of Courtenay's captured followers, three were transported to Australia never to return, others served prison terms of up to a year with hard labour. The last armed insurrection in England was over, but the memory lingered on. As for Grace – an imagined character – what had she to look forward to? Perhaps a life in menial service, of sad memories and an unfulfilled potential, a fate suffered by many of her sisters in the nineteenth century.

TALE EIGHTEEN

The Painter Man

Moving ten years on to 1848 the excitement stirred by 'Mad Tom' had abated whilst conditions for the rural poor were gradually being alleviated as enlightened self-interest amongst the well-to-do became more fashionable. The countryside around Harbledown retained its distinctive character in spite of the closeness to Canterbury. In the village itself and out towards Upper Harbledown some new houses had replaced old cottages and farms. The population had almost doubled to seven hundred and seventy since the beginning of the century. The area's picturesque rustic charm had begun to attract men and women of wealth, distinction and discrimination, those who wished to enjoy being of the city but not living in the city . . .

Tom glanced furtively out of the dame-school window, catching sight of the London-bound coach as it slowed to take the bend in the road. "Lucky them," he thought, envious of the passengers riding on top, clinging to the firmly tied trunks and baggage. It was a hot, sultry day and in the distance he could hear the low rumble of thunder. His stiff collar chaffed his neck and he felt itchy and uncomfortable, not helped by sitting near to the window, catching the afternoon sun. The elderly teacher's voice droned on and Tom wriggled on his hard seat. He was nine years old and for him, now, on this July day in 1848, school was the last place he wanted to be. The only thing he really liked doing at school was drawing but that was a rare treat as paper and pencils were expensive and sketching on a cracked slate with a lump of chalk was frustrating. Still, he would soon be ten and able to leave this stuffy room forever and be free, free to learn a trade, earn some money, grow to be a man.

Tom lived at Harbledown with his father, mother and two smaller sisters in a cramped cottage just off the London-Dover road. His father was a cottage weaver who made a steady living, selling his finished cloth to a draper down in Canterbury. The city at this time had already expanded beyond its ancient walls and the age-old ribbon development along the main roads leading into it was pushing further out into the surrounding fields. The coming of the military in the Napoleonic wars and the building of cavalry, artillery and infantry barracks had much to do with this growth. On the other side of town, away and up-wind from the city smells, fine officers' houses had been built in St. Dunstan's Terrace, facing out over open fields towards Harbledown. Behind the terrace were the close-packed, small houses in New Street for their batmen and coachmen. In-filling had started and new roads began to enclose the fields off the main highways. Harbledown itself saw change with the enlargement of Hall Place by its new owner, the Countess of Athlone, and the splendid terrace of houses built on Summer Hill, commanding a stunning view out across the city. To be high and healthy were much sought after qualities for the better-off especially if they desired to raise a family for parts of Canterbury were renowned for their unsavouriness. The area called Northgate was now much connected with the barracks, with streets of small, poor, terraced houses, lots of brawling public houses and, it was generally agreed, a number of brothels. This was probably true down the ages for many of the pilgrims of earlier times were not all holy-minded.

It was in the crowded parishes down by the riverside where fevers, chest and rheumatic illnesses were most common and where, over the centuries, the pestilence struck. This was not surprising given the damp soil, the profusion of small back-yard abbatoirs, the numerous ancient graveyards, and the absence of piped water and a proper sewage system in these lowly neighbourhoods. Sometimes Tom went to visit his Aunt Alice who lived in Duck Lane and more than once was forced to cover his nose because of the stench rising from the pools of stagnant, filthy water as he picked his way along the unmade lane. In summer the river smelled as well and the better-class citizens kept clear as much as they could.

There was another side to Canterbury, though. Many rich merchants and tradesmen, as well as eminent clerics and the garrison officers and their ladies lived in and around the city. For them the top end of the town, with its landscaped Dane John Gardens, its military bands and fashionable parading, was much more pleasing to their taste – and safer.

The city had Assembly Rooms, a dancing school as well as a Philosophical Institute and a lively if provincial social life. Unfortunately, Canterbury was run by a small closed-circle of wealthy men who corrupted local politics for generations to come, seeing everything in terms of personal self-interest rather than the general public good.

There were however, individual men, and women, of conscience who fought long, lonely but dogged campaigns to improve the health and education of Canterbury's poor and needy, not least Dr. George Rigden and the brothers George and Sidney Cooper.

None of this was known to Tom, for mainly he knew only what he saw and was told. His world was much fixed by his father's work, the daylong clack of the loom, often well into the night, by the school room, by the monthly walk down into Canterbury with visits to the markets and his Aunt Alice. He would stand and watch the soldiers march by on parade – or run and dodge and leap out of the way of passing coaches and carts. He had learned to read but there were few books to hand, only the family bible but that was old and the print small, with muddling letters that made his head spin. He much preferred to be out and about, off through the orchards and hop-gardens, up in the woods, catching rabbits for the pot, looking for bird's eggs, even collecting blackberries. Tom had one special place. It was a narrow stream down through the hop-gardens, close to where the main road bent to climb towards Upper Harbledown. Here he spent hours, paddling, building small dams, watching for sticklebacks and other tiny fish, catching the occasional frog, looking out for dragonflies.

He had to be a bit careful not to be spotted and chased off. Any small boy out in the orchards or hop-gardens was immediately judged to be up to no good, although old Fred, who worked this land, often pretended not to see the boy crouched hiding in the bushes. There was a sort of unspoken agreement between the two, Fred would see but say nothing providing Tom didn't do any damage or draw attention to himself.

When school finally ended that hot afternoon, Tom called in at the family cottage for a quick drink of water and to rip off his stiff collar. He shot off to his stream, promising his mother to come home straightway if the storm broke. It was with immense relief he sat on the bank, took off his heavy boots and thick woollen socks and paddled his feet in the cold water, wriggling his toes. As he sat he gazed up at the clouds slowly drifting across the sky, huge, white, flat-topped mountains piling high, but with ominous black-grey bases. As he watched, making pictures out of the clouds, the sky over Bigbury began to darken and a flash of lightning flickered in the distance, followed by a growling rumble of thunder. The air was still and swarms of midges rose over the stream. It was so quiet, Tom thought he could hear them singing. He sat perfectly still, absorbed.

It was then that he heard the sound of approaching footsteps. Grabbing his boots and socks he began to scramble to his feet, ready to dive into the nearby bushes but as luck had it as he turned he slipped on the muddy bank and fell flat on his face. There was a laugh and a man's voice said, "Hold up, my lad. No need to run off. I've been watching you for some time. You seem to be in a day-dream. What were you thinking about? Come, let me help you up."

A hand reached down and hauled Tom to his feet. There in front of him stood a slenderly-built man, with a thin, drawn face. He was dressed in plain clothes and wore a wide-brimmed hat. Slung over his right shoulder was a leather bag brimming with pieces of paper and pencils, whilst from his left hung a bulging canvas bag.

"Here, let me put these weights down for a minute." The man eased his bags onto the ground and gazed around."This is a very pretty spot you've chosen for yourself, young man. Do you live hereabouts?"

Tom eyed the stranger suspiciously. What was this man doing here tramping through the hop-gardens? What was in those two bags? And what about that broad-brimmed hat?

"I live just up the road, sir, in Harbledown village. This is my best place, where I come to see things."

"See things, hmm. So you like seeing things, do you? What sort of things do you mean?"

"Well, sir, the fish, the insects, frogs, rabbits, those great clouds up there. If I had paper and pencil I'd draw them. I like drawing."

The stranger laughed. "So do I, so do I. But I like painting them even better, especially cows and sheep and dogs. Not easy, but they give me great pleasure and some profit. Are there any cows around here? I've been tramping around all day but all I can find are hops and orchards."

"I know where there are some cows, sir. Close by, but you'd have to walk that way," said Tom, waving his arm towards the river meadows. "There are some sheep, but they're over the back of the church. Do you want me to take you there?"

By now Tom was feeling much more confident as here was a grown-up prepared to talk with him, not chase him off as a nuisance.

"That would be kind of you," said the stranger, smiling. "You see I am what they call an artist, a painter. I am staying in Canterbury with my mother for a short while and I've decided to re-discover the countryside I knew as a boy. So here I am. My, but this is a splendid spot. I wouldn't mind living here."

At that moment there was a great flash of lightning with an almost instant echoing clap of thunder. Heavy raindrops began to fall from the rapidly darkening sky.

"Come now, we'd better find shelter," said the man. "It's dangerous out here in a storm. And we won't take cover under any trees. Where do you think we can find somewhere safe and dry?"

"Follow me, sir", and Tom led the way, both of them jogging up through the hop-garden. They ran, the rain pelting down as the storm broke around them. Jagged bolts of lightning forked into Bigbury woods, the thunder cracked and rolled round the hills.

"Quick, quick sir!" panted Tom. "Look, there, that old shed, we'll be safe in there."

Half an hour later the rain ceased and the wet and chilled pair emerged into sunshine.

"My, look at that rainbow," said the stranger.

Arcing across the sky was the most vivid sight Tom had seen, not one but two rainbows, the nearer faint against the dark purple clouds out towards Thanington, the other sharp and clear and multi-coloured. The man and boy stood awestruck until suddenly both rainbows faded and disappeared as the sun clouded over again.

Tom led the stranger to his home, saying his father would be angry, and please would the kind gentleman explain how he had been caught out in the storm. The stranger took the initiative and introduced himself to Tom's parents.

"My name is Thomas Sidney Cooper and I want to thank you for the kindness and good sense shown to me by your son, Tom. He was civil enough to stand talking with me, answering my questions. That is how he was caught in the storm. I am much obliged to him for finding me somewhere to shelter."

At these words Tom's parents instantly thawed and invited Mr. Cooper in for a warming cup of tea and a chance to dry out by the kitchen range. They fell to talking, as grown-ups do, about the weather, the state of trade, how things were not as they should be. Then Mr. Cooper turned his attention to Tom. "That's a good, sensible boy you have there. He tells me he is to leave school soon. What plans have you for him, if I may ask?"

Tom's father explained that the boy was to be apprenticed to his uncle in Faversham, cask-making for the brewery. A steady, skilled trade which would see him well. But that wasn't until next January and until then Tom would be looking for odd jobs, helping where he could.

"Excellent," said Mr. Cooper. "I wonder if I might employ him until then? I've a mind to walk more hereabouts when I come down from London and I shall need a guide. And someone to help me with these." He kicked the two bags at his feet. "That reminds me, we might as well finish what's in here." With that he emptied out the canvas bag: a piece of ham, a hunk of bread, cheese, apples and a small flagon of ale. "Would you be pleased to join me?"

So it was all arranged and for several weeks during that summer and autumn Tom met up with the Painter Man, carrying his bag and leading him along little known tracks through the orchards, hop-gardens and woods and down to the river. More than this, Sidney Cooper provided him with a tablet of drawing paper and assorted pencils, encouraging him to draw and giving helpful advice. Come Christmas, it was time to end the contract between them and Tom was delighted to receive a set of paints and brushes from the great man. By now the family had learned how, in spite of his humble origins, Sidney Cooper was widely travelled and held in high esteem in London where his pictures were regularly shown at the Royal Academy. And how Her Majesty, Queen Victoria herself, had recently commissioned a picture by him.

Two years later Sidney Cooper became a Harbledown resident for during that autumn with Tom he had taken his brother George on one of his walks and shown him the spot where he had met the boy. To Sidney's delight they discovered this particular stretch of hop-garden was for sale and soon he had purchased four acres. A year later he began building a small gabled cottage, designed by himself and an architect friend. As the years went by he added further adjoining land and built extensions until the cottage had become a large house. It stood in thirty-two acres of magnificent landscaped gardens, with a rich variety of trees and a small wooded island marking the spot where Tom had his 'secret place'.

Sidney Cooper became a wealthy and influential man, holding a series of dinners and banquets for city dignitaries at his great house called Vernon Holme, named after his friend and patron, Robert Vernon. More than this, he helped the city by founding an Art School in 1867, next door to where he had been born and grew up in great poverty with his deserted mother and four brothers and sisters. He built a theatre, donated public open space, and he and his brother helped James Beaney, a local labourer's son, to study medicine at Edinburgh. Many years later Beaney himself became a city benefactor, founding the Beaney Institute. Sidney Cooper lived in Vernon Holme until he was ninety-nine years old, painting almost to the end.

Living in Faversham and later in South London, Tom grew to manhood, learning to be a cooper and raising his own family. He never forgot that magical summer when he was ten and still kept his drawings and paintings from those days, even though they became faded and the edges curled. From time to time he read about Sidney Cooper, his fame and good deeds and although Tom sometimes passed the great man's house when visiting his aging parents now living in Canterbury, he never dared call. Such things were not done. But Tom knew how it was the Painter Man, as he still thought of him, really came to Harbledown.

Tom is fiction, as is the meeting with Sidney Cooper. The details of Cooper's rise to fame and the growth of Canterbury and Harbledown are fact. Vernon Holme is now used as a school but the trees planted by Cooper and his son flourish. The Art School building Sidney founded is now much used for community and adult education activities but may become an Arts Centre. Sidney Cooper is increasingly recognized as one of the great British artists of the 19th century for both his landscapes and animal paintings. He lived from 1803 until 1902 and left an unequalled record of Canterbury and rural life spanning nearly three-quarters of a century.

TALE NINETEEN

The Rector Wronged?

The nineteenth century rolled on into the twentieth century and then in 1914 came the First World War. Changes had accelerated. Railways arrived at Canterbury, from Ashford in 1846 and from Faversham in 1860. Roads were improved, local government reformed (especially important in corrupt Canterbury) and public health and education were introduced. The advent of railways saw a shift back to fruit growing for the London market in and around Harbledown, but the hop-gardens remained much in evidence. The seasonal round of farmwork continued but now London families came by train to help with the hop picking. Canterbury grew, especially out along the main roads, Old and New Dover roads, Whitstable Road, and London Road, with in-filling between by large and modest Victorian houses. Within the city walls and in the St. Stephen's, Northgate and Wincheap areas and particularly out along the Sturry Road, terraces of modest villas and small houses appeared, some replacing older dwellings. The city's population doubled between 1801 and 1901 whilst Harbledown parish reached a total of nine hundred and ninety-four at the turn of the century.

In Canterbury, brewing, milling and leather making were dominant, with thirteen breweries and over one hundred public houses, much in use on the weekly cattle market day. Canterbury developed its own brand of provincial life, with Cricket Week marking the apex of the social calendar. Out in the countryside agriculture continued to dominate but old houses had been refurbished and enlarged, new grand ones built. Harbledown still had its personal character although the sunken main road up Church Hill now had a high brick retaining wall on one side. Over on Bigbury greedy men nibbled into the side of the old hill-fort for gravel but its mass resisted their efforts and soon they were off, looking for easier pickings. Back at St. Nicholas' Hospital the 17th century almshouses were replaced in 1840 by stone-built single-storey cottages with the Frater meeting house restored at the same time. St. Michael's also underwent restoration and extensive alterations. Rectors came and went but one made a lasting impression . . .

The Pepper family were just sitting down for their tea when there was a thunderous knocking on the front door. Harry, the youngest, jumped up to see who was calling, opening the door gingerly. To his surprise, there stood the elderly Rector of St. Michael's church, the Reverend Charles Hairby Barton. A short, stooped figure, clad in clerical black, his face was angry and intense.

"I want to speak to your mother, my boy!" he snapped, pushing Harry to one side and entering the house.

"Excuse me, Mr Barton," said Maud Pepper, stepping forward, blocking his path. "I don't recall inviting you in. Be pleased to step outside. We shall talk there. And mind your feet on my fresh-scrubbed doorstep." For all her diminutive size, Maud was a feisty woman, mother of six, left widowed by the Great War and not overawed by anyone. Especially not this aged Rector.

"Now sir, you seem to have a problem. So tell me."

"It's your lad there, young Frank. He had the impudence to knock my hat off. I want him dealt with."

"That's as maybe but no one lays a hand on my children, other than me – and don't you forget it! Frank, come here. What's this all about? And mind me, I want the truth."

"Well, it's like this. Yes, I did knock his hat off, but you should have seen what he did to me."

"So, tell me," Maud said.

"I was riding my bike down the hill when Trigger, sorry, Mr. Barton there stuck out his stick and poked it into my front wheel. He was walking in the middle of the road like he always does and saw me coming. He did it on purpose and I went straight over the handlebars. That's how I got this big bruise. When I got up he was walking on as if nothing had happened. So I went up and knocked his hat off. Sorry, ma."

"Well, Mr. Barton, now we know. Young Frank here shouldn't have knocked your hat off and for that we all apologize. But if you carry on acting in such foolish ways, for all that you're our Rector, you'll be in serious trouble. No wonder people talk about you behind your back and do you down at every chance. Now, good evening to you." And with that

130

she shut the door firmly in his face. The children all suppressed their giggles for Ma was mighty cross.

The family lived in Harbledown, the end house in a small terrace. It doubled up as the village post-office. Life was not easy and never had been, even when their father, Arthur Henry Pepper, known to everyone as Harry, was still alive. He had originally come here from East Sussex and married Maud Jordan, who came from Berkshire and was in service at Hopebourne. Harry ended up for eighteen years looking after the horses for Lt. Colonel Cordeaux who lived at Hopebourne. Harry supplemented his earnings as an ostler by acting as the village postman, whilst Maud went in to cook whenever the Lt. Colonel held one of his grand dinner parties. The children all attended the small, three-roomed, stone village school, erected in 1853 on land purchased from St. Nicholas' Hospital. It was less than fifty yards away from home. The headmaster was a Mr. Gomm, a nice man, but the children all feared Miss Hitchens' special arm-smacking punishment. It left your arm red and sore for several hours after. They called her "Scratchy 'Itchens" behind her back. Bill, the eldest son, was the first boy from the school to win a scholarship to the Simon Langton school, much to the surprise and envy of some of the locals who thought such a thing not possible. But both his brothers, Frank and Harry, did the same, confirming that intelligence did not depend on wealth and status. Sadly, the three girls, Vi, Maud and Elsie, were not given the same encouragement.

For the six children Harbledown was a good place to grow up in, even though there was never much money to spare for treats. They had Duke's Meadow, the fields, orchards and woods to roam in, and apple scrumping was part of the way of life, although you had to be careful not to get caught. A great dare was to go into the empty house called The Hermitage after dark. It was held to be haunted. Sundays were something of a bore, including two church services and a walk uphill to the tin shed at Upper Harbledown for Sunday School, both morning and afternoon. But there were always the horses father looked after, including the great horses who pulled the wagons.

The boys especially, cadged rides down from the paddock to the stables. There was also the chance to go swimming in the River Stour, a walk across the fields towards Thanington. And in winter time, if there was enough snow, there was tobogganing on Duke's Meadow. Some remembered how in the fierce long winter of 1895 the then Rector had produced a great sledge shaped like a boat which carried seven or eight youngsters at a time, but it had been hard work pulling it back upslope.

At that time hop-gardens spread all around but the family never went 'hopping' as it was called. Their mother always thought such work beneath her dignity. "Nasty, horrible, dirty, smelly, itchy work," she called it. Not only that, she had something of a prejudice against the poorer families who walked out from Canterbury to help in the hop-gardens on Hospital Farm, and an even greater prejudice directed at traveller groups and folk from the East-End of London. "Drunkards all," she would say. "Spend the whole day making their wives and children work and then drink it all away at the pub in one evening."

Her children knew this wasn't at all fair for they made many good friends with youngsters from the hop-picking families but their mother had some very fixed opinions. Beneath her toughness she was, however, kind-hearted and generous-spirited and went out of her way to be helpful to those in genuine need. The children enjoyed the annual influx of these noisy, cheerful 'hopping' families with their huge bonfires and singsongs, the back-chat, the occasional fist-fight, the ways they tried to cheat the Tally-man, the sense of hustle and bustle around the place. By contrast there were the early mornings when mist hung low over the hop-gardens and woods, muffling sound and causing the bines to drip as if it were raining. The London families arrived by train to Canterbury where they were met by wagons by the farmer at Upper Harbledown. It was a fascinating sight as the wagons, loaded with pots and pans, bits and pieces of furniture, bags and boxes and small children passed through the village on the way to the hopper huts up the hill. There was a pattern and a rhythm to life.

Then, in August 1914, came the Great War. In 1916 Harry volunteered to fight for King and Country although at his age he could have stayed behind. He was first in the Royal Engineers but ended up in the Gloucesters, helping plug the gaps in the infantry torn out by campaign after bloody campaign. For the children the war was a time of both hardship and hunger but also of great excitement. Soldiers were billeted all round the village and a mobile anti-aircraft gun to fend off any attacking Zeppelins was stationed behind the houses on Summer Hill. An aeroplane crash-landed on Golden Hill, whilst Hall Place was taken over by the military. Soldiers drilled in the main road before moving off to France. Then there was young Hughes, from up in the Mint, who finished up in the Royal Flying Corps, a hero to the local lads.

For Harry there was no such fun. He survived the blood and stench of trench warfare right through to just seven weeks before the conflict ended. He was killed early on the morning of September 29 1918, in the battle for the St. Quentin canal, just a week after baby Harry was born. The stunned family received a lengthy letter, reprinted in the *Kentish Gazette* on October 12, from their father's platoon officer. It was more than the standard expression of regret at his 'truly noble and heroic death' for it included a fine compliment which talked of Harry's splendid example to the younger lads in the platoon and how he looked after them in trying circumstances. It also spoke of him being struck by a bullet and dying instantly. Just eight weeks later another letter arrived, a bill from the War Office for the blanket in which his body had been buried.

It was only years later when the Regimental history was published that the family learned of the kindly-meant lie told them. Harry had been detailed to go out with a young lieutenant and a small squad on a probing patrol, ahead of the main British bombardment and attack. It was a still but foggy morning, wet and slippery underfoot. The patrol had weaved its way out, through the barbed wire, across no-man's-land, ducking and sliding from water-filled shell-hole to shell-hole, slithering across a sunken lane only to be met by a random burst of German machine-gun fire. Harry had been cut down and severely injured and had to be dragged back, moaning and groaning, dying slowly and in great pain. The young lieutenant was able to report the first attack objective was strongly held by enemy machine-guns. But this was known already so nothing was served by Harry's death.

At five minutes to six that morning the rolling British barrage erupted and the attack, over the top, was underway, both men and tanks fumbling forward in the thick fog, the air deafening from the shrieking shells, the whistling of bullets and the crack and crump of exploding shrapnel shells, mingled with the tack-tack-tack of machine-guns. Because of the fog, the attack stalled and it wasn't until midday, when the sun broke through, the advance got underway again. By the time darkness fell the Gloucesters had taken their three objectives, a few hundred yards of churned up no-man's-land and some abandoned German trenches at a total cost of eight killed and forty-seven wounded. Harry had been one of the eight dead. He was later buried at the British cemetery at Vadecourt, one of the million British servicemen who died in "The war to end all wars". A total of twenty-seven men from the Parish of Harbledown were killed in the Great War, a tremendous blow to such a small community.

That was now all in the past, five years before. It was now

late February 1925, and Harbledown was changing. The main road carried increasing amounts of traffic, the occasional car, a few omnibuses, lorries and vans as well as jolly groups of cyclists. Horse and carts and farm wagons still puffed and panted up and over the hills. The village remained separated from Canterbury by fields but large houses had spread along London Road almost reaching the foot of Summer Hill. The village itself had consolidated, with sturdy brick-built houses perched overlooking the road as it cut into Church Hill. The once scattered cottages and farms half a mile away towards Dunkirk were now bound together by newer infills with Harbledown Lodge and its park giving some status to what was called Upper Harbledown. Up on the edge of the Blean woods increasing numbers of houses and a few bungalows made up the emerging Rough Common community.

Canterbury itself had crept out along the main roads and was a thriving market town with light industries, mostly associated with agriculture, and its tannery and flour mills. Still a garrison town, the Great War had brought increased prosperity, and now the East Kent coalfield, only a few miles away, was adding a new economic dimension together with miners and their families drawn from all over the coalfields of Britain. Improved transport meant more shoppers and bigger shops, whilst the Cathedral had begun to attract increasing numbers of visitors, both by train and motor bus. The High Street was busy and bustling, still carrying all the two-way traffic from Dover to London. In summer it was dusty and fly-ridden even though the water cart trundled back and forth spraying several times a day. In winter it was wet and mucky underfoot.

Canterbury was where you went to senior school, to hospital, to the dentist, to the cinema, to the market, to catch a train, to buy new boots or dresses. It was where the work was if you wanted to be other than a farm labourer – and there were fewer and fewer full-time jobs available on the land. And it was also where you went to see a lawyer, to appear in court, or to go to goal.

It came as no real surprise to Maud Pepper and her children to learn that Rector Barton was to appear before the St. Augustine's Petty Sessions in early April. For a long while now there had been considerable disquiet amongst some of the parishioners at what they saw as the increasingly eccentric behaviour of their Rector who had been in office now for twenty-four years and had married several times. As far back as May 1919 there had been an editorial in the *Kentish Observer* complaining about "the pitiful state" of St. Michael's churchyard, how the tombstones were almost hidden by weeds and grass and commenting on the fact there had been no church-wardens or a sexton for several years. This was not entirely surprising as so many of the local men had gone off to war, never to return, but even so it suggested something was amiss.

And now this. The Rector was accused of entering the churchyard on the evening of 21 March 1923, and attacking the recent tomb of Mr. George Clouette with a hammer, knocking off a sundial which he then threw away. At the Petty Sessions there seemed enough evidence from two eye-witnesses, a young courting couple, Elsie Petty and Donovan Buckland, to send the case forward to the Kent Quarter Sessions in July. Meantime, another scandal involving the Rector rocked the village. A local J.P., Charles Hardy, who lived at Odsal House, accused the Rev. Barton of pocketing half-a-crown from the communion service collection. This charge was thrown out before it reached the Quarter Sessions.

At the Quarter Sessions, in spite of the evidence of the two young eye-witnesses, the jury took little time, not even retiring, to bring in a "not guilty" verdict. Elsie and Donovan were quite clear what they had seen at 6 p.m. on that Spring evening. They knew and recognized Rev. Barton, so they recalled, as he came into the churchyard, not least from his distinctive rapid, short-stepped walk but also by the bowler hat he always wore. He was carrying a hammer and muttering to himself. He first went to Mr. Edender's tomb, and hit the kerbstone several times. Then he walked back up the path to the Clouette tomb, knocked the brass sundial off, picked it up and threw it in the bushes, commenting: "Look at that hideous thing!"

The defence lawyer made great play of how reliable or otherwise the evidence of a young courting couple could be, especially at dusk whilst under a tree in the churchyard. Perhaps they were too preoccupied to have seen clearly who it was. This caused much tittering and elbow-nudging in the courtroom. Heavily guided by Lord Harris, who was overseeing the court proceedings, the "not guilty" verdict was virtually instant. There were those who said it was all a white-wash to save the Church authorities the embarrassment of admitting years of neglect over the St. Michael's affair. There were others, however, who thought the Rev. Barton had been framed by someone or some bodies who had a grudge against him. "Well, that would likely be some of the gentry-folk who don't like the Rector's views," said Maud, knowingly.

It was soon after the court appearance that a number of the leading local families decided to break away from St. Michael's and hold their own worship in St. Nicholas' church. They even talked of hiring their own preacher to conduct the services. Bill and Frank left the St. Michael's choir and transferred to St. Nicholas' but after a couple of weeks decided what was going on was silly. They gave up the choir altogether.

Within eight years the Rev. Barton had gone, but was not forgotten for at Christmas in 1927 he had set up a Trust with £1,250 to give quarterly help to four needy regular church-going parishioners. The board detailing his generosity still hangs on the church wall, alongside the memorial he funded commemorating those who were killed in action in the war, a lasting reminder of a controversial Rector who may well have been wronged.

The incidents mentioned in this story are based on family reminiscences, articles in local papers and relevant documents. The three Pepper brothers left Harbledown in turn to join the Royal Air Force as regulars. All served in the Second World War, Bill in France, escaping after Dunkirk, Harry escaping from Singapore, and Frank, shot down over France in early 1940, a prisoner-of-war until released by the advancing Red Army in 1945. Two of the daughters, Vi and Maud, became nurses at St. Augustine's Hospital whilst the youngest, Elsie, was apprenticed as a hairdresser. Bill Pepper is my father, his parents, Maud and Harry, my gran and grandad.

TALE TWENTY

The Birthday Present

Through the nineteen twenties and thirties Canterbury remained a quiet almost sedate market town, marred by the occasional Mosleyite Blackshirt march. Increasing traffic up and down the congested High Street gave an impression of busy activity, especially on market days. In some ways, however, it was a period of stagnation and relative decline with contracting industry. Even so, beyond the old city walls there was a wave of housing development, especially ribbon growth out through Blean toward Whitstable, also on the Ashford Road at Thanington, to the south and east, with off-shoots from the main roads eating into farmland and orchards. There were even a few Council estates beyond the barracks. Harbledown remained separate and much unaltered except for Rough Common which grew apace. Bigbury, still a mix of coppiced woods and orchards, saw new, secluded houses appear.

Down in the city some things changed, with new large stores like Marks and Spencers appearing, a car-park in Broad Street and four cinemas opened. For the most part it stayed a city with buildings ranging over eight hundred years in age and appearance, close-packed family shops, narrow lanes, ancient churches, crowded backstreets, pubs galore, a scattering of public buildings and, above all, the Cathedral and precincts dominant and seemingly everlasting. Then the Second World War began on 3 September 1939 and with the fall of France and the Battle of Britain in 1940 Canterbury became a front-line city, less than forty miles from the Nazi bomber bases . . .

It was a funny old way to spend the start of your eighth birthday, huddled here in this musty, smelly, brick air-raid shelter, for what seemed hour after hour, listening to the German bombers droning overhead. Reggie was so bored sitting here in the lamp-lit shelter he took to counting all

137

the different sounds he could hear: the sniffling of old Ma Baker in the corner, the wheezing cough of Uncle Alf, his older sister Muriel clicking her fingernails, the subdued talk of the grown-ups. He wanted to be outside, looking at the sky. That's where it was all happening, well, most of it.

Old Jerry was really having a go this time. Reggie could hear the far-off shriek and crump of falling bombs, the crack of the anti-aircraft guns, the occasional whoosh of the recently-arrived rocket battery nearby. If only he was outside, up the lane at the top of Summer Hill, he could watch it all happening – the criss-cross beams of searchlights, the bright white light of the parachute flares, the flashes of ack-ack in the sky, probably tracer-bullets too. With a bit of luck there would be plenty of shrapnel bits and pieces to collect when the raid was over. As for Canterbury, he couldn't imagine what it looked like. He had stood on the hill looking down over the city after another, smaller, raid, but then all there was to see was a column of black smoke. Tonight was different. The sirens had wailed out sometime before midnight, including the three rasping blasts of Tugboat Annie, meaning a raid was imminent.

"And on a Sunday night too!" his Mum had complained. It was now two o'clock in the morning, Monday June 1 1942, his birthday. "Happy birthday, Reggie," his Mum had said as they bundled into the shelter built at the bottom of the lane and until now not much used.

Reggie sensed all the grown-ups were really worried this time. There had been a lot of air-raid warnings over the past two years, mostly after the German fighters had nipped in low and undetected, using the Water Tower at the top of St. Thomas' Hill as a landmark before sweeping in down over the city, all guns blazing, occasionally dropping a bomb or two, then off and away. "Hit and run" they called it. Reggie had once been down visiting his Gran in Orchard Street when there was a sudden roar of aircraft engines and three Messerschmitts, one after the other, skimmed the roof-tops of the big houses in St. Dunstan's Terrace. Reggie, who was playing out in New Street, could see their machine-guns flashing as they sped by and the silhouette of one of the German fighter pilots. He knew they were Messerschmitts, just as he could tell the different sounds the German bombers made, whether they were Junkers 88s, Dorniers or Heinkels. He had first heard the distinctive thrumming roar of Messerschmitts when they bombed those strange, secret aerial masts up the road at Dunkirk back in August 1940. He was later to learn these were amongst the first radar masts in the world and played a crucial role in the British air-defence system.

It was a few months earlier in 1940 when he had his first real awareness of how serious the war was, again at the time of his birthday. He had been staying with his Gran but had gone down to the railway level-crossing in St. Dunstan's Street. In those days it was thought, and was, quite safe for a six-year-old to be out on his own "providing you keep out of the road". Playing in the street was part of every child's heritage and right. On that particular day all the grown-ups were very glum and anxious so he thought he'd go and watch the trains go by. That was always fun with the great steaming, smoking engines clattering and clanking by with their distinctive sharp, smutty smell. But on this day there were more trains than usual. The gates across the road seemed closed most of the time.

He stood there, watching with fascination and some excitement. Train load after train load crept by, all heading towards Ashford. They were crammed with soldiers, many hanging out of the windows waving but not like any soldiers he had seen before, like the ones marching proudly and smartly in the big parades. These were men dressed in tattered bits and pieces of uniform, some had blankets round their shoulders, others had bandaged heads or arms in slings. They looked a scruffy but oddly cheerful lot. There was something else strange. On the wind he could hear a far off rumble like very distant thunder but it never came any nearer. Close to Reggie, standing watching the trains go by, was an old man. To Reggie's surprise he was crying and kept saying, "Our poor lads, our poor lads."

Reggie went back to his Gran's and told her what he had seen and heard. She told him about what was happening at a place in France called Dunkirk, how the men he had seen had been rescued and brought back, to Ramsgate she reckoned. And the thunder? The sound of the guns from across the Channel. "A lot of brave men are dying today," she said. Reggie nodded, stored this information away, and went out to play.

A few months on, late in August and into September the skies over Harbledown and Canterbury brought the war even closer. It was the Battle of Britain being fought out, the R.A.F. against the Luftwaffe, the "Few" against the "Many". For Reggie this had been another time of high excitement. He would lie on his back in a cornfield just over Mill Lane watching the white vapour trails weave and curve across the blue sky, sometimes picking out the pin-prick specks of fighter planes and bombers, diving and wheeling, sometimes seeing one fall out of the sky, leaving a thin pencil-line of black smoke. Most of the time it was, for him, a silent battle, although once he had a narrow shave, which he told no one about in case they made him stay indoors, when a spent cannon-shell zinged down into the ground a couple of feet away. It was still hot when he picked it up to add to his collection, an old Oxo tin box full of bits of jagged shrapnel, spent cartridge cases and the pin of a hand grenade given to him by one of the young soldiers billeted with his Gran. Sid was his name and the last Reggie saw of him was when he and his platoon cheerfully marched off down Orchard Street for France. But that was ages ago.

Sitting curled up in the shelter he had fallen half-asleep, lost in thinking about his hoped-for birthday presents, not that there was much to choose from. Everything was rationed and toys now were mostly hand-made out of scraps or second-hand. He roused up as Uncle Alf loudly cleared his throat and said, "It's all gone quiet. Perhaps it's over. Ought to be, it's nearly three o'clock and I want my bed." Then the all-clear wailed.

Reggie jumped up. "Let's go up the lane, Mum. It's my birthday. Oh, go on." His mother reluctantly agreed but made his fourteen-year-old sister Muriel go with him. She didn't want to and started grumbling about it not being fair and why should she. "Because I say so, my girl." And that was that.

Reggie raced on ahead. It was still a bright moonlit night but the sky towards Canterbury was glowing red. As he panted out onto the main road he stopped, transfixed, for there below was a scene he would never forget. It looked as if the whole city was on fire, red, yellow-white flames shooting and sparking into the sky, great clouds of smoke, grey in the moonlight, drifting across the valley. Even from here he could smell the burning buildings like a great bonfire. The silence was eerie. As his eyes adjusted to the garish glare he began to pick out familiar landmarks – the top of the Westgate Towers, the Cathedral still standing but strangely lit from burning buildings all around giving it a dusky-rose colour. There was Bell Harry tower, wreathed in clouds of smoke.

Suddenly, up over the hill from behind him he heard a vehicle approaching, then another and another. A column of fire-engines, ambulances, lorries and some cars sped by, heading for the inferno. These must have come from Faversham or further, he thought. His feet itched to run alongside them but his sister kept a firm grip on him. Even she seemed taken-aback by the fire-filled valley below them.

Reggie became aware that a whole crowd had now assembled, even old Ma Baker, all standing looking, some weeping quietly.

"Those poor people," said Mum. "Hope to God your Gran's all right. It looks to me as if this side of the river missed it but you never know. You children stay here. I must get down straightaway to see if she is all right. Come on Alf. Now, back home to bed, you children, right now. And don't forget the blackout."

Reggie dozed off but was up by 5.30 a.m. His mother had returned, Gran was fine but a bit put out. "You know what she's like." Apparently Uncle George had spent most of the time standing out on the pavement wearing his A.R.P. tin-hat, smoking Woodbine after Woodbine, looking up at the sky, ignoring the shrapnel which fell around him and refusing stubbornly to get into the shelter.

"Silly old B. Just like him to make your Gran furious," his mother said.

"Well I suppose as it's your birthday you'd better go and see your Gran. She was asking when to expect you so I said after breakfast. Lucky for you there's no school today. But don't go wandering off. Straight there and straight back."

Reggie certainly went straight there, as fast as he could, down the hill, now crowded with vehicles of all kinds heading for the town, taking the long path across the fields past the rec to the top of Orchard Street. On the way he passed groups of people, pushing prams, carrying bundles and suitcases, trudging out of the ravaged city, heading for the safety of the nearby villages. He stayed with his Gran for an hour or so, putting on as polite a face as he could amidst all the comings and goings of anxious friends and neighbours. Eventually, clutching a chunk of his Gran's special cake, he managed to slip away but instead of heading for home, he cut across the railway bridge, through the field down to Whitehall Road to get to the Westgate Towers.

Here was another unbelievable sight. Fire engines and lorries were parked all over the road, people were scurrying about, many in uniform or overalls and wearing tin-hats, but all strangely quiet. A mass of hosepipes covered the roads snaking through the Westgate Towers, up into St. Peter's Street. Glass and fragments covered the road and pavements and crackled underfoot. Some shops and houses were windowless, others were already being boarded up. Reggie sniffed. The air was thick and heavy with the smell of burnt timbers, scorched tarmac and rubber. A white-grey, sharp-tasting ash carried on the breeze and made his lips feel dry. He started to walk on but found his way blocked by a lanky, smudge-faced man in overalls and a tin-hat.

"Where do you think you're going sonny?"

"Goin' to have a look, mister. See if I can find a bit of a bomb. It's my birthday."

"Well, Happy Returns to you too, but you're not going anywhere except home. Not today, matey. You don't want to go up there," he said, waving towards the top of the town. "That's a right mess and no mistake. Jerry meant business last night and just like him, he'll be back, I reckon."

Reggie's face fell. The man laughed and said, "Hang on a sec." He returned after a couple of minutes and handed Reggie the tail end of a German incendiary bomb. "Now take this and buzz off." Reggie could hardly believe his luck. This would be the best thing yet for his collection. He sped off back to Harbledown, the prize possession hidden under his jacket. Now that was what he called a real birthday present!

The characters except for 'Gran' and 'Uncle George' are imagined but the events are real, based on the author's own childhood experiences in Canterbury 1940-42. The Luftwaffe returned again to bomb the heart of Canterbury on 2 June and 6 June, retaliation for the R.A.F.'s thousand-bomber raid on Cologne. Much of the historic core of the city was destroyed but thanks to the unsung and mostly unrecorded gallantry of the Cathedral air-raid wardens the "Great Church" was saved.

TALE TWENTY-ONE

Where Has All The Magic Gone?

After the Second World War the devastated parts of Canterbury underwent major reconstruction, much of it inferior in design and character, so much so that fifty years on a new wave of redevelopment is underway. In more recent years greater care and attention has emerged, making use of planning powers to try to ensure some sense of style although in certain cases a Disneyland pastiche has predominated. There have been benefits. A new ring-road around most of the old city wall enables the main street to be pedestrianized, the A2 by-pass takes heavy Dover and London-bound traffic away from the city, leaving it to be enjoyed by a million tourist visitors a year as well as untold numbers of shoppers. The tyrant of the motor car has only been partly challenged and the city suburbs suffer from on-street parking and rat-running. These new suburbs result from a wave of house building in the 50s, 60s and 70s, with large-scale infilling by Council and private estates, including the London Road estate, butting right up to the edge of Harbledown, as does the Westgate Court development, just falling short of Duke's Meadow. Nearby stands the huge Kent University complex, high on the valley side, overlooking the city. Below, light industry and commerce has spread either side of the city, along the river flood-plain, once avoided because of the danger of seasonal inundation.

Within Harbledown parish there have been few and only small-scale developments, some infilling, some conversions, mostly at Rough Common. Hall Place had been rescued, along with Odsal House, but at Upper Harbledown an ugly garden centre mars the local scene. There are other blemishes on the skyline but fortunately no electric pylons. The Harbledown by-pass carves a groove behind the old village, severing it from Rough Common and Upper Harbledown but relieving it, after two thousand years of major through traffic. Orchards now predominate with hop-gardens becoming fewer and fewer. The great Blean forest still

143

dominates the horizon and seems well protected. Virtually the whole of Upper and Lower Harbledown are now Conservation Areas, recognizing their historic and architectural importance. Bigbury remains much unknown, even to some of those who live there. It has yet to have a large-scale archaeological survey and dig to reveal more of its true nature and function. The ancient trackway, now called the North Downs Way, still passes through it. Much remains from the past but the threat from those who are ignorant of their heritage or who put profit before all else in the name of progress is ever present. The future of Harbledown, like its past, is in our hands. If we fail . . .

The two cousins, Charlotte and Amy, turned off the electronic guided toll motorway and drove into the Harbledown Centre, the Golden Pyramid it was called. They had decided to make a day trip, a visit back to the cottage where their Gran and Grandad lived, in the Mint, down by the side of St. Nicholas' churchyard. They had been talking about old times, sorting through photographs and video clips, laughing and teasing about how they looked when they were small, the strange fashions and hair-styles of those days.

It was now A.D. 2020 and both were in their early thirties, living in a country which had somehow lost its way in spite of all the advances in technology. The ethos of market forces now ruled every aspect of life. After the failure of the New Model Labour Party to come to power in the late nineteen nineties, the process started in earlier years had been finally brought to fruition by Michael Portillo, now known as the Lord Protector. The Royal Family had fallen so much in public esteem its members were merely ciphers, visible only when they hired out their services for some great function or the opening of new complexes or shopping malls. Shopping had become the key leisure activity which brought people out of their homes.

The National Health Service was no more and like all the other public services, except for the Lord Protector's bodyguard, had been privatised. Education, the fire service, the police and the armed forces had all gone the same way. Local and regional government had been abolished, not least because all their powers had been stripped away and there was nothing left for them to do. Instead there were Lord Lieutenants or High Sheriffs with executive powers, answerable only to the Lord Protector. Even Parish Councils had been scrapped, replaced by local commercially sponsored Citizens Watch Forums, talking-shops mainly for the elderly but with no powers – or so the cynics said. For there were still cynics, those who queried and questioned what was going on, those who talked longingly of the "good old days". But these were a dying breed for most people now scarcely had time and energy enough to care for themselves and their family, let alone worry about laughable concepts like concerned neighbourliness, community, the needs of others or even society, whatever that might mean.

As the two young women had approached the turn-off to Harbledown they had already noticed changes from their childhood. The roadside was lined with flashing advertising holograms, blocking any view, not that it mattered for once on the toll-way the automatic drive took over and there was nothing to do but watch the scenery pass by, mainly desolate, scrubby farmland, golf courses, theme parks and pleasure-tels, places where you could drop in, tune in and flop out, caught in day-long virtual-reality fantasies. They had managed to catch a glimpse, high up on the Blean wood skyline, of a series of stumpy projections, exclusive dwellings called "Keeps", built in mock-Norman style for the very rich and each standing in its own patch of ancient forest.

They parked their vehicle at the garish Centre, standing where once had been what the locals called the "Golden Triangle", a piece of unused ground which some in their naivety had wanted to turn into a nature reserve. That was before most planning controls had been abolished. First came a motel and filling-station, then a tourist hotel and night-club, now a twelve-storey pyramid complex which included a shopping mall – "The Golden Pyramid". Opposite, across the by-pass they could make out the flashing entrance to the five hundred time-share cottage "Leisure village" which, according to the big-screen talking advertisement, had its own golf-course, clubhouse, entertainment centre and exclusive woodland bridle paths.

"I remember there used to be a farm, just over there. And a pretty walk through the woods," said Amy.

The cousins made their way on foot, first making sure they each had their personal security systems fully charged, the stun rod and electronic shrieker, both essentials in these days of danger from the UCs, the underclasses, the poor, desperate and lawless ones who did whatever they could to survive in a land where the Welfare State was a distant dream. Both young women were fully paid-up subscribers to SECCAL, short for Security Call. This entitled them to summon up assistance in the event of trouble, an all-inclusive service not only for personal security but for breakdowns, injury and fire. "Pay or you burn" was one of the slogans.

As they walked along the weed-grown, cracked footpath they immediately commented on how the hillside field where they remembered seeing free-range pigs lumber about was now covered with chalet-style dwellings, perched on stilts and rising in serried ranks.

"They must have a fine view," said Amy. But Charlotte pointed out towards Bigbury. "Not any more. Remember how Grandad used to go on about that, what was it?, that Iron Age hill-fort. That's new, whatever it is." Bulking up on the Bigbury skyline was another huge building, all reflective glass and gleaming white concrete.

"I remember seeing this on the vid-net," said Amy. "It's the new Brazilian tech-research estab. You know, the one they've funded as part of their bid to buy out the University."

"Well, I suppose we call that New Age instead of Iron Age," came the rueful reply.

They made their way past what used to be Vernon Holme school, now returned to being a private residence. But there was a difference for it was surrounded by high-tec security systems and there was an armed guard at the gateway. He waved them on with his lazer-stun pistol as they paused to peer at the house. It was the same with the guard at Hall Place for all pedestrians were suspect as now only the poor walked anywhere and to be poor was to be labelled potential criminal. The other half of the population buzzed about in their mini-drives, small, secure personal electric-powered vehicles. All the railways had long been closed down except for a few heritage lines operated for tourists. Even the Channel Tunnel was no more, too expensive to rebuild after its destruction by a terrorist suitcase nuclear bomb. They noticed Hall Place was now an exclusive guest-house for Chinese tourists. From the hologram ads it seemed it was decorated, furnished and run in mid-nineteen forties style, a period of British history which, for some reason, fascinated the Chinese. Cutting out uphill alongside the house was a gleaming highway, recognized from the antique but vandalised signpost as the A28 by-pass. This swept out on stilts over the valley towards Bigbury.

The two young women jogged quickly through the smelly underpass, stun rods drawn. This was just the sort of place you found lurkers. Emerging they were both shocked to see Hopebourne had gone.

"That's where great-great-grandad and gran worked, didn't they?" asked Amy. Now, instead of the house there was the entrance to a shopping entertainment complex which covered acres of what had been Hospital Farm orchards. A vast extent of jumbled building styles, linked

146

by footpaths lined by stunted fruit trees, spread before them.

"At least they've kept the oasthouses. Remember how we used to walk down past them to get to the stream. I suppose that's where that artificial lake is," Charlotte said.

"I liked those orchards. They were fun. Look, there's the old church, St. Nicholas' isn't it?" asked Amy. "Let's go up the old pathway, up the side there, where the old well is. But what's that gate-house doing there?" As they approached the medieval-style gate-house they saw the sign: "The St. Nicholas' Leper Hospital Heritage Experience". Slipping their combined identification-charge cards into the slot they entered, to be met by a man dressed as a monk, in a long brown habit and sandals, his tonsured head gleaming in the weak sunshine. "Welcome my children, welcome," he greeted them in an oily voice. "Just walk on and see, see what was here, brought to you by Heritage Hospitals plc." By now all charitable trusts had been wound up by government edict at the turn of the century and forced to become limited companies with the duty of making money for shareholders rather than giving it away.

Stifling their laughter, the young women walked up the path, amused to see it was covered with artificial dung and rubbish. They paused at the old well, now made much more of a feature with a surround of artificial stone-work, draped with plastic hop-vines. The water bubbled and seethed, giving off steam.

"I don't remember it doing that when we used to come here to play," commented Charlotte. "This must be some sort of tourist scam. And I used to think this was a magic place." Sure enough she was right for a hologram figure of another monk suddenly appeared, hovering over the well, inviting them to purchase phials of holy water before they left.

As they turned into the church grounds a bizarre sight met their eyes. The old stone almshouses had been transformed to look like ancient wattle and daub thatched cottages and there were about a dozen or so men and women, dressed in what they assumed were replicas of what lepers wore, pretending to dig and hoe artificial herb and vegetable gardens. One, noticing their presence, stepped forward, ringing a bell and holding a pouch out on the end of a stick. "Alms, alms for the unclean," he requested, flicking his hood aside to give a momentary glimpse of a grey-white ravaged face.

"At least the make-up's realistic," giggled Charlotte. They made their way to the Chantry, now the heritage centre's shop, wondering whether to buy any souvenirs, repro pilgrims' badges, miniature leper-bells, even stick-on grotesque leper face-masks and sores.

147

"Go down well at the next children's party," commented Amy. "Come on, let's get out of here. What about the church?"

They went into St. Nicholas', even though there was an extra fee to pay. "Well, they can't do much to spoil this, or can they?" said Charlotte. But they had. As the pair entered, a piped medieval monks' chant began and suddenly the mock candles came alight, filling the old church with a flickering light. An unctuous voice-over began to describe the church and its history, with hologram figures flitting about, portraying important persons from the past, Archbishop Lanfranc, the Black Prince, Henry II and others. Then the lights went out, leaving them momentarily in pitch-darkness. "And now, for your delight, our fabulous reinstated church murals." Spotlights came on as the wall-curtains slid back and there, in breath-taking colour, were the murals, covering the walls.

"Now that was worth seeing," said Amy. "Pity about all that other rubbish."

The two left by the side gate out into the Mint, noticing that it was security coded and that the whole church grounds were surrounded by the ever-present safety system. So too for the cottages in the Mint. They saw that most had now acquired extensions or dormers jutting out of the roof, some tastefully designed, others a hotch-potch of plasti-wood shacks and sheds.

"Didn't Gran tell us this was a Conservation Area?" asked Amy.

"But they did away with them twenty or so years ago," came the reply. "Now people can build what they like, how they like. Remember Grandad telling us once people forgot how to respect their environment and their neighbour's rights then we'd all end up living like selfish animals. He said we'd all be safe in our high-tec personalized cages, afraid of everyone else and not caring for anyone except ourselves. Well, he was right."

"I used to like the view out the back of the cottages. Do you remember all those orchards and trees? But look, down there, it's still covered by that complex you get into where Hopebourne used to be. And where that ends there are all those boring-looking houses. What a waste." Amy bit her lip, looking sad. Charlotte nodded her agreement. "Let's walk up to Golden Hill, that looks as if it's still open land."

On their way they passed the guarded gates leading into Harbledown Park, noticing the same again for Lanfranc Gardens. As they got to the top of Mill Lane, passing along the footpath from Summer Hill, they saw the warning sign.

"Don't tell me this has become a no-go area," said Amy. "Looks like it. Come on, let's keep moving."

They reached the way into Golden Hill only to find it too had a security gate, with a charge for admission and vid cameras perched on poles to keep watch.

"Seems like the National Trust can't trust anyone anymore," said Charlotte. "Still, let's see what the view is like." But they wished they hadn't, for there spread out before them was a sea of buildings, interspersed with patches of greenery and parking lots. Canterbury had finally enmeshed Harbledown, the countryside had been swallowed up and all in the name of individual freedom of choice and the accountant's view of life which calculated the cost of everything and knew nothing of the value of anything.

Saddened and upset Charlotte and Amy decided they'd seen enough. One last visit though, down to the Victoria rec, but there they found the children's play area a weed-covered, vandalized wreck and a charge for admission to the open space, now privatised and called the Victoria Pleasure Gardens. Back up the hill, past the barred and closed-off St. Michael's church and graveyard, now all crumbling and overgrown, for a final look at Duke's Meadow, well Duke's Park as it was now named, exclusive dwellings, each in their guarded, high-walled enclosure. And so to their car, both now silent, remembering what had been, what could have been kept, what had been lost. They agreed never to come back. Nor did they. For them the magic of Harbledown had been lost, squandered because no one really cared enough to stop it happening whilst there was still time.

But we know it need not be so. There is still time to save Harbledown and its magic. We do not have to betray our grandchildren. The choice is ours. Let's keep the magic.

This is something of a worst-case scenario but one which projects forward trends and characteristics found in Britain and elsewhere in the mid nineteen-nineties. We must try to ensure this fantasy, or any part of it, remains fantasy and never becomes fact. Be warned!

ACKNOWLEDEGMENTS

The information used in the Harbledown tales comes from many and varied sources: from Caesar's *De Bello Gallico* to Edward Hasted's monumental *History of Kent*, from Marjorie Lyle's recent *Canterbury* to Audrey Batesman's *Hail, Mother of England.* Other works which have proved most useful are: *The Battle in Bossenden Wood* by P. G. Rogers, Frank Jessup's *A history of Kent*, Tim Tatton-Brown's *Canterbury: history and guide*, *The Peasants' Revolt in 1381* ed. R. B. Dobson, and Walter Norris' unpublished *Some notes on the history of Harbledown.* Especially helpful were the church guides for both St. Nicholas' and St. Michael's, Harbledown, together with numerous articles and reports produced by the Canterbury Archaeological Trust. My warmest thanks go to my father, Bill Pepper, for his childhood reminiscences.